The BRAVE 🍁
COURAGE DURING COVID

FOREWORD BY SUSAN STANDFIELD

Copyright © 2021 by Lionheart Publishing

The Brave: Courage During COVID in Canada/Multiple Authors – Volume 1

ISBN: 978-1-7775400-1-2

All rights reserved. No part of this publication may be reproduced, distributed or transmitted in any form or by any means, including photocopying, recording, or other electronic or mechanical methods, without the prior written permission of the publisher, except in the case of brief quotations embodied in critical reviews and certain other non-commercial uses permitted by copyright law.

DISCLAIMER: This book is for entertainment and education purposes only. It is not intended to serve as business advice. This book is not intended to instruct or advise in any way. Using any of the information in this book is based on the reader's own judgment after consulting with his or her trusted professionals. The views expressed herein are not necessarily those of the publisher, nor the other co-authors. The resources provided in this book are based upon the recommendations of each individual author and may change or cease to exist without notice. Further, the systems, techniques, and suggestions presented here may have been successful for the co-author, but the reader may not receive the same results or any results at all. All company names and product names are copyrights of the respective owners. None of the owners of products or services mentioned herein have endorsed this publication; they are simply mentioned as examples of resources that the reader might find helpful. While all attempts have been made to verify the information provided herein, the publisher assumes no responsibility for errors, omissions, or misunderstanding on the subject matter. The reader assumes full responsibility for their own actions with regards to their use of this information. No guarantees are made.

Lionheart Publishing
Website: www.fenixfallgirl.com
E-mail: lanigelera@hotmail.com
Instagram: @fenixfallgirl

Dedicated to
The Brave

This book is dedicated to all of the BRAVE Freedom Fighters, Truth Seekers, Justice Warriors, Community/Rally/March Organizers and everyday proud sovereign Canadians who have chosen to stand up to government corruption, speak out about medical fraud, and question absolutely everything they are being told about COVID-19 by a manipulative, fear-mongering, false mainstream media narrative.

By sharing your brave stories during COVID-19 in Canada, you will inspire and empower a nation to courageously take back our sovereign health and rights from a communist dictatorship. Your righteous actions and valid voices are being heard and making bigger waves around the country than you will ever know.

Thank you for defending our
Canadian Charter of Rights and Freedom and working toward the future we all want and envision with Peace, Unity, Prosperity, and Love for all!

Table of Contents

FORWARD BY SUSAN STANDFIELD	7
1. LANI GELERA - A Course in Courage	10
2. SUSAN STANDFIELD - The Third Jeep	19
3. KRISTEN NAGLE - Canadian Frontline Nurse	32
4. ALICIA CHRISTINE JOHNSON - Fearless	42
5. KIMBERLY NUEDORF - Brave Story	50
6. JODI LYNN - To Be Brave	59
7. SARAH CHOUJOUNIAN - A Voice for the Voiceless	72
8. SHERRY ROY - Brave Story	80
9. PAUL ALLEN - The Courage to Rise Up	87
10. AMANDA FORBES - The People's Truth	99
11. KATY SINHA - Brave AF	110
12. DANIELLE ELISE PISTILLI - For Many Are Called	120
13. CAITLYN RICHER - Standing Out From The Crowd	135
14. TANIA KAHZAAL - Faith Over Fear	142
15. DR. DENA G. CHURCHILL - Fuel Purpose	151
16. MARK FRIESEN - Spirit of Rebellion	162
17. AMANDA MOSES - Courage Through the Darkness	171
18. TANYA GAW - Action4Canada	182
19. ELENA BUTLER - Freedom Thinkers Community	191
20. KAJA GJESDAL - Spiritual Warfare	205
GRATITUDE FOR THE BRAVE DONORS	217
ABOUT LIONHEART PUBLISHING	219

Foreword by Susan Standfield

Of all the human traits, bravery might just be the most important going forward. Compassion, yes. Open-mindedness, certainly. Humour, without question. Those are all highly valuable human traits that make life worth living. However, bravery holds a unique and timely space for all Canadians right now in the spring of 2021, to challenge us to rise up despite our fears so we can all be brave in the face of growing tyranny. Being *brave* is how we're going to win our freedoms back, one person, one voice, one moment at a time.

So what exactly is bravery? How does it manifest, and how can we nurture this crucial human trait? Most people may not have paid much attention to bravery in Canada, as we've enjoyed one of the highest qualities of life on Earth for many decades. We have, until now, been mostly a rich and free nation protected from tyranny by our social and intellectual institutions, which are now under vicious attack. We've not needed to be very brave. All this changed last March when our government chose *not* to protect our freedoms. Swiftly, the process began of removing them in collusion with foreign and domestic shareholders in a highly organized scheme of crime known in legal terms as 'by proxy high treason,' occupying Canada in a Coup D'Etat. Some of us were brave from the start when we saw this happening; others have stepped into their bravery over the last thirteen months.

This is what I know about bravery.

Bravery is the outward expression of the human soul calling out to safeguard others in moments of crisis. These moments can be bold and striking, or they can be tiny and hushed. There is no rulebook for bravery, no qualifying degree or list to follow. It is quite simply the dormant emotion of justice that lies within us all. We are all brave somewhere inside of us, which is why this book is so important. I was extremely honoured to be asked to contribute to *The Brave;* I knew immediately it would become a catalyst for change in Canada to inspire others to step into moments of their own bravery one person, one moment at a time. Story has the power to do that which is the archetype of the hero, the one who shows bravery in the face of adversity or injustice and inspires us to believe in humanity despite great odds surrounding us all over the world.

Bravery is the child in Africa who walks hours a day to a makeshift schoolroom so they can receive an education. Bravery is also the parent who foregoes seeing their children so they can put food on the table. And bravery is the woman who drops off clothing to a woman's shelter. These are moments of bravery when we think beyond our personal needs and act for the benefit of humanity, and it is the foundation of all human rights advocacy, to use ourselves no matter what the consequences so we can help and protect others.

This beautiful book is full of stories of people who have expressed unusually high levels of bravery over the past year to expose the fraud of COVID in Canada. We have been silenced, shamed, assaulted, slandered, disowned, arrested, stalked, and humiliated by a system so corrupt it seeks only to protect it's self-interest and not us, everyday Canadians who are now victim of it. Every person in this book was chosen for their incredible story of bravery, and I hope you take the time to read each one slowly with contemplation about how you, too, can be brave despite any fears you may have.

As you read these stories, you may think *I couldn't do that,* and I assure you yes, you can. None of us thought we could do the things we have done for more than a year, but we did. We still are, and we are all much stronger and more humble people as a result of our acts of bravery. That is one of the very unknown results of bravery – humility – because it softens us and forces us to connect with others in ways we never did before. Bravery is an incredible

Foreward by Susan Standfield

privilege and honour and, should you be ready to step into your own moment of bravery, you too will be forever changed for the better.

When I started the No More Lockdowns lawful protest march movement on April 12th, 2020 at Vancouver City Hall, I had no idea how brave I would be forced to become and how compassionate the experience would make me. What I did know was that someone had to tell our story one day, which is now happening thanks to Lani. Her book series is a natural evolution of our exploding human rights movement across Canada, and it's going to create a known and lasting record of our efforts. This is extremely important in human rights work, that others bear witness to injustice and those who stand up to protect others. In humanitarian work we call this 'temoignage' or to bear witness. Now we have this record. All of our bravery is going to travel yet again around the world thanks to Lani inspiring a whole new generation of people who will begin to step into their own bravery so they can protect themselves and their loved ones.

If you want to be brave but think you're too afraid, try to remember this ... the moment you speak out, the instant you go into action, you will be forever changed for the better, and you will never be afraid again. In fact, you will know what every person in this book also knows – that you were only afraid of fear itself.

Let your soul guide you. That is where all bravery dwells.

Susan Standfield

Chapter One

A Course in Courage

By Lani Gelera

As a Courage Coach, I teach people how to be brave in all aspects of life. I'm passionate about helping others process and consciously face their perceived fears. Teaching people to be brave and learn how to believe in their authentic selves with self-love and integrity is what a Courage Coach does. Our greatest fears in life often have the greatest lessons to teach us individually and are, almost always, in alignment with one's path and purpose. I've always believed that we are all forged by the fire, and we are never presented with more than we can cope with and learn from at any given time. It has become my mission to discover the teaching, the consciousness, and the mindset we can develop from overcoming our own adversities. The question I seek to answer is: what makes someone brave?

What is it about their life experience and acquired knowledge that gives them the confidence and conviction to stand up against corruption, tyranny, oppression, and injustice? Why do some people feel compelled to put their career, business, relationships, or their lives on the line in order to fight for freedom and what they believe is the truth?

What does it mean to be "Courageous"?

The word *courage* comes from the Latin word "cor," or the French word "la coeur," which means the heart or the center. Courage means to come from the heart. Whenever we speak from the heart, act from the heart, or stand up and fight for something we love and value, we are being courageous. Courage is not a physical act; it is any act that comes from the heart. Courage is a mindset. It is a choice we make in the face of a perceived social threat or physical danger. It comes from a tenacious spirit and a discerning moral compass. Courage almost always comes from the intuitive guidance and instinctual drive to do what is right, what is just, and what is necessary to move forward and not only survive, but also thrive. Being courageous, whether conscious or not, is an act of love.

It was March 11th, 2020 when I gave a talk at the local Squamish Adventure Center for the Chamber of Commerce. I was asked to emcee the event and talk about being "Courageous in Life and Business" with four other prominent thought leaders in the community. I opened the evening on stage, joking about asking anyone concerned about the virus to politely curtsey in front of me if they didn't want to shake my hand. Everyone laughed at the silliness of it all. There were over one hundred local community members in attendance, and we enjoyed what we didn't know was to be my last public speaking event that year.

Only a few days later, the COVID-19 pandemic fell upon the entire planet with a wave of fear-mongering by all major mainstream media channels around the globe. As the world, my country, my province, and my community started to shut down and close in on me for two weeks to flatten the curve, I sat back and watched in utter bewilderment as almost everyone fell into the lower vibrations of fear, panic, and despair.

Falling into Fear

I watched with abhorrence as my hometown Squamish locals became horrible to outsiders and would scream unwelcoming and cruel obscenities at anyone they thought to be not from around here. "Go the F home!"

they hollered. All because of their fear. I couldn't wrap my head around the logic of hoarding toilet paper or the concept of panic buying more than you needed, just in case, leaving others to go without.

Over the next few weeks, we collectively rode the ridiculous roller coaster of COVID-19 restrictions and regulations as the mainstream media, the government, and the "health professionals" started explaining that we were no longer "allowed" to see our families. I was no longer "allowed" to date a stranger. We were not "allowed" to hug certain people unless they were in our household. We had to stand six feet apart from everyone else and, ultimately, it was recommended we all start covering our faces. If we were caught breaking any of these new COVID-19 regulations, Bonnie Henry, our unelected BC Health Minister, would suggest we publicly shame, condemn, gaslight, and rat out our neighbors and report any delinquents to the police. All these violations to our Canadian Charter of Rights and Freedoms were implemented under the guise of a national emergency and in the name of safety and the lives of our beloved grandparents.

As the COVID-19 signs, plastic dividers, spots to stand on, and arrows to show you where to walk all became commonplace and seemed uncomfortably permanent, I began to realize that there was no going back to the normal we once knew and longed for. Nothing would ever be the same again. And, if we didn't start fighting for all the rights and freedoms that were being taken away under false pretenses, we would lose them forever and fall into a future of communism and draconian control.

From day one, I knew what fear-mongering looks like and the purpose of intentionally making people afraid. People are easily controlled and manipulated when they are living in fear. I know what propaganda is and how the mainstream media is really good at pushing an agenda or a false narrative. I worked in television/film for twenty years as a stuntwoman in Hollywood North. I could see right through all the bullshit, the lies, the fake news, and the underlying intention that was being perpetuated. I just didn't yet know why.

Red Pilling the Masses

In April 2020 I saw *Out of Shadows*, a documentary by two professional stuntmen in Hollywood, one of which I knew and had worked with on a few movies. This documentary was a glimpse into the behind-the-scenes Hollywood lifestyle that very few ever get to talk about and live. It was a true account of the nature of Hollywood and the purpose of celebrities, movies, and television. Mike Smith and Brad Martin did an amazing job of red-pilling millions around the globe with regard to MKUltra mind control, Mockingbird Media, Pizzagate, and the CIA involvement in Hollywood. I messaged Brad immediately and told him this documentary is going to wake up the world. I thanked him and wished him and his family well.

Those of us who were consciously "awake" to the 3D matrix questioned everything the media, the government, the politicians, the medical industry, Bill Gates, Fauci, Trudeau, Tam and Bonnie Henry said. And those who believed everything they were told were swept away in the fear porn of an intelligent and deadly virus that everyone was transmitting and most definitely would kill your loved ones if you dared to breathe fresh air in public.

I have been a compassionate, considerate citizen most my life and always strived to make a difference and contribute to my community. However, I was not going to be held personally responsible for the poor health choices and compromised immune systems of others if they, by chance, contracted what appeared to be the flu. None of these new provincial orders and rules were ever passed through a court of law. How could any government entity demand that I not visit my friends, my family, my loved ones, and then accuse me of being selfish when I chose not to spend all of my time alone? None of it made sense to me. My intuition told me there was a nefarious agenda behind this entire fake pandemic. Then, Bill Gates miraculously announced he had the only viable solution to save the world.

Having grown up most of my life without vaccinations, I valued my immune system function and natural remedies and medicine. I am an Energy Healer, and I believe in our own divine ability to heal ourselves from sickness and disease. I also believe in divine purpose and that absolutely everything happens for a reason. I have never believed in vaccinations, and I knew the Bill Gates proposed vaccination had nothing to do with a flu virus. They were going to try and commit genocide. According to the Georgia Guidestones, the New World Order Agenda was to depopulate the planet and control future fertility to maintain a population under 500,000,000.

Discerning the Truth from a Lie

When you believe and trust in yourself, you will know intuitively who you can believe in and trust. Once you understand the NWO agenda, you will be able to discern the truth from a lie in every single action, statement, and narrative they propagate across the globe. It all becomes crystal clear.

The separation of the wheat from the chaff was becoming apparent as the entire planet started to shift from 3D lower vibrations into the 5D higher consciousness and awareness. This was obvious for anyone who had eyes to see and had not surrendered their rights, their freedom, and their own free will to the mind control tactics of a corrupt and tyrannical government system.

Having fallen down for a living for twenty years as a stuntwoman, I consider myself brave. Not only physically brave, but more importantly and practically, morally brave. I have stood up to those who have tried to oppress me and push me down. I have spoken out against those who have tried to shut me up and tell me my voice doesn't matter. I have chosen to courageously fight for the things I love and not against the fears that would otherwise control me. I have overcome childhood adversity and learned how to heal, how to forgive, how to discern the truth from a lie, and how to embrace the values that are most important to me in my life. I do feel brave, and I'm not inclined to sit down, shut up, do as I'm told, obey, comply, or conform. That is not in my nature. I'm a Leo.

If you don't stand for something, you will fall for anything.

When the television/film industry started up again in late August/September, I was called back to work for dozens of stunt days. Of course the new draconian COVID-19 regulations and restrictions were in place with mandatory masks, social distancing, testing two to three times a week, and COVID-19 Marshalls watching your every move and interaction like the gestapo. I have jumped off buildings, fought off five monsters at once, and fully lit myself on fire on a runaway horse carriage. But not once, in my twenty-year stunt career, have I ever been asked to compromise my integrity, discard my personal values, and do something I did not want to do for a paycheck. Well, maybe I was asked to, but I never ever did. I have never sold my soul to the devil for fortune and fame. I chose to turn down all the work that was offered to me until this entire fake pandemic hoax was over. Only then, if there was anyone left who wanted to hire me, would I fall down for a living once again.

Having an abundant mindset and believing in my divine path and purpose, in the fall of 2020, I set out to help humanity with the ascension of our consciousness. I was determined to help all those who wanted to build a brave and abundant mindset. I created my Lionheart Activation Journal, a thirty-day journaling challenge to shift your mindset into a higher vibration with courage, compassion, authenticity, and integrity. This book was designed to assist those who wanted to start working on their own personal growth skills and spiritual development.

Teach These Ones To Be Brave

The best way I know of to teach others to be brave is to show them examples of The Brave. That is the purpose of this book. *Courage During COVID* is to become somewhat of a "Course in Courage" for Canadians. It will also become a true account of what has actually transpired during this fake pandemic and attempted global genocide. These are not the stories that will be shared by the mainstream media. These stories are the truth. This book will become a part of our history and a tribute to all of those who stood up, said something, and took action in the face of government tyranny and medical fraud.

I believe most people are paralyzed by their fears and unable to take action mostly because they do not know how to stand up and advocate for their own health and freedom. They do not know what they can do to speak out with all the censorship in a cancel culture. They do not know what their sovereign rights are that are being violated. Most of the country has been so indoctrinated, programmed, and told what to believe most of their lives; they are not even aware of what their own true values are. How can you stand up for what you believe in and fight from the heart for values that you have not even defined for yourself? What are your values in life? What is most important to you? What are you willing to fight for?

In this book, I have compiled twenty brave authors from across the country who are courageously sharing their story of standing up for themselves, their rights, their freedom, their families, and their future. With various perspectives, some of these stories are of truth seekers, freedom fighters, health justice warriors, rally organizers, Canadian frontline nurses, chiropractors, spiritual leaders, correction officers, mothers, and business owners. They will share their mindset and what has compelled them to take action from the heart, be brave, do something, and be the change they want to see in the world. What makes them any different from the rest of the country living in fear? What makes them any different from you?

These brave authors will compassionately speak from the heart and share their fears, their loves, their losses, and their victories in this battle between the dark and light forces. These are the stories of the brave and will become an essential part of our collective understanding of how we collapsed the corrupt and evil systems that were no longer working and transitioned into a higher dimension, the New Earth, the Great Awakening, and the Golden Age of Humanity.

About Lani Gelera:

LANI GELERA survived a childhood of emotional trauma and adversity. She then grew up to be an independent, confident, and courageous professional stuntwoman in Hollywood North TV and Film. After falling down for a living for twenty years, the concepts of overcoming and facing fear, developing authentic self-love and self-respect with integrity, and standing up for her beliefs and values were forged into every fiber of her being. Her connection to spirit reminded her how divine and powerful she truly was, and she aims to share that remembrance with the rest of the world.

Lani is a Courage Coach, an Energy Healer, a Light Worker, and the CEO of Lionheart Publishing. She is a best-selling author and has been writing for adventure magazines, blogs, and articles for the past six years. Assisting humanity in elevating our collective consciousness and vibration with courage and compassion is, without a shadow of a doubt, exactly what she is meant to be doing at this point during the Great Awakening of Humanity.

Instagram: @fenixfallgirl
Facebook: Lani Gelera & Fenix Fallgirl Adventures
Website: www.FenixFallgirl.com

Chapter Two

The Third Jeep

By Susan Standfield

My story of choosing leadership to expose COVID-19 and public health fraud in British Columbia using my face and name

MY BACKSTORY
Hanging out with other moms on my kids' school playground in the posh West Point Grey neighbourhood of Vancouver, I was shocked to learn I was being threatened with a $250,000 fine and six months incarceration because I had no intention of ever handing over my two kids' vaccine records to the BC NDP government. *WTF?* I thought. This kind of legislation exists in BC in 2018?

It was then I began what has been a three year journey to learn who was motivated to threaten mothers like me who chose not to inject our kids with unsafe toxins. *Who would benefit from threatening me?* I wondered. Who had the financial motivation to enact such an injurious and criminally-minded piece legislation targeting me? Who held the power to get Janet Austin, BC's current Lieutenant Governor, to sign it? Most strangely, why was Lana Popham, the BC NDP Minister of Agriculture's, name on it? Her fiduciary duty and salary was supposed to be focused on food, so why was she approving vaccine policy? None of this made sense to me. All of it was suspiciou

The answers to my question arrived three months before what I call "The Great Corona Heist of 2020." As I stood screaming in the school hallway clutching the pharmaceutical marketing colouring book I had wrenched from my six-year-old's backpack the day before, an unusually forthright school employee enlightened me that it was the Public Health Officer of BC who held absolute unchecked power. Under the School Act, a crime had been committed against my daughter, and I demanded to know the reason why. That moment and that person put me and my family on a far safer trajectory than we had previously been on, and I will be forever grateful for their candor, professionalism, and guts to give me the truth, which others were not willing to do.

Since 2018 I have studied how bureaucrats inside the BC government have weaponized the entirety of BC's political, media, and judicial institutions to benefit the people I discovered were threatening me – pharmaceutical shareholders – in collusion with public health officials and the myriad of "authorities" who increasingly dictate our lives. That is a whole other story with many books to be written on how BC has become an epicentre for pharmaceutical investment, lobbying, policy, and human test subjects, like my children who were exploited and trafficked by the sick care industry to profit off the overall decline in our health. It's nothing less than a shocking horrendous nightmare, especially to someone like me who grew up in the 1970s when we lived and thought far more freely and naturally in BC. I am a living testament to the benefits of that lifestyle both mentally and physically. I don't even have a family doctor. British Columbians are getting sicker, sadder, and now much poorer thanks to the corruption of public health in British Columbia.

BLATANT FRAUD

Along with that rather unique and unmarketable skill set making me a complete social pariah, in March of 2020, I also had thirty years of credentials working in the media, mostly American television advertising, making commercials for the biggest brands in the world including, you guessed it, Big Big Pharma. So when I watched Bonnie Henry, BC's Public Health Officer, step in front of the first CTV camera to speak at her first Daily Health Update press conference, I knew exactly why she was there, who had written her script, and every lie coming out of her mouth. It was never about "natural" health; it was only ever about "public" health, and there is a huge difference. What I saw was a highly paid pharma-backed population surveillance expert with a comforting voice and welcoming school teacher attire acting on a stage with most of the five million British Columbians in her audience falling for her fraudulent performance. These viewers consume BC media so regularly they have no idea how often they are lied to. I knew how often because I used to make those programs, and a huge chunk of the money that drives this industry now in BC is from the same shareholders who targeted my children at their school – Big Big Pharma.

Earlier, in 2018, I had come across science that tipped me off to the evil within pharma. I stumbled upon the General Electric website and found $750 bottles of Fetal Bovine Serum half the size of a litre of Coca-Cola. FBS is the blood drained from baby cows while they're still alive inside their mother's womb, a key ingredient in manufacturing vaccines for its purity and ability to duplicate cells. I knew that blood could contain traces of agrichemicals, vaccines, steroids, and god knows what else the mama cow had been fed, and I knew those chemicals could cross the blood brain barrier of children. Bang! It hit me like a truck. This was the exact same intentionally lax regulatory framework that killed my mother thirty-two years earlier when I was eighteen and she was fifty-four. Big Tobacco had used doctors to lie to her in their ads to promote smoking to women like my mother so successfully, they eventually destroyed her life. Regulatory consumer warnings only went on cigarette packages seventeen years after she died, thanks to Canadian shareholders who lobbied *against* these safety measures. I realized in that moment, staring into the immense wealth of GE, that I had the moral obligation to speak out and protect others in a way I was not able to when I was young. I couldn't help my mother because her addiction was stronger than her will to live, and my family never recovered from her death because of failed health policy in Canada.

CHOOSING LEADERSHIP

I call my kind of activism "flak jacket activism," or in war terms, The Third Jeep. The Third Jeep is a famous anecdote that describes how armies approach enemy lines successfully. When an offense is launched in a ground war, who moves forward in what order is highly tactical. Surprisingly, you don't send your strongest forces out first or even second. You send them out in "the third jeep," after the enemy has heard the engines of the first jeep and pointed their guns at the second jeep. It's the third jeep at which they take aim, so those forces need to be the most fortified because they face the heaviest of fire and often don't survive. This is where the most fatalities occur unless these forces have adequate protection, something I realized I had in spades. From education to poise, influence to compassion, and most importantly, having lived and worked all over Africa for most of the last twenty years, I knew I could outsmart the people lying to five million British Columbians. I chose leadership because I knew I would be stronger than most people. I had the cunning and weaponry to dodge and survive every bullet fired in my direction, which there have been many over the last fifty-two weeks since I began.

The other big reason I chose to lead was where I had come from and how I was raised. This gave me even more firepower in the fight against corrupt governance. I grew up on the west side of Vancouver in a neighbourhood called Shaughnessy. I'm the daughter of a high profile lawyer/part time property developer and a nurse/banking executive, who retired when my older brother was born in 1966 because that's what moms did back then. Our family friends were supreme court judges, lawyers and bankers, and I was actually a debutante, which only a few boyfriends and my old friends know about. These days admitting such an act of exclusive social ritual would be considered the ultimate in white privilege, which I get. Of course I understand that. But this is the world I was born into and a very real reason I chose activism for part of my life's work; I know how powerful wealthy circles operate and how to disrupt them because I was raised within them. I guess you could say I come from a part of "the cabal" which is what being a debutante is all about.

When I was seventeen, I was granted entrance to Vancouver's affluent society in front of Queen Elizabeth's 1986 representative in British Columbia, Lieutenant Governor Bob Rogers. I know how absolutely ridiculous this sounds, but at the time it was normal to me, and my mother believed it would help me shake my inner troublemaker tomboy. I was taught ballroom dancing lessons, how to eat and socialize during seven course meals (rather handy during intel-gathering espionage, by the way), and of course how to curtsey in front of royalty in preparation of my big day, the cotillion or ball.

Six months later, all packed to start my first year of political science to earn my Bachelor of Arts from Queen's University, I hopped on an Air Canada flight to Toronto. I said goodbye to my mother, whom I imagined I might never see alive again. She was wearing a wig after rounds of chemo to get through the last four months of her life. I waved goodbye in YVR Domestic Departures, slung my backpack over my shoulder, and walked through security crying. This was probably the most defining moment of my life, knowing I was going to have to teach myself everything about being a woman. As it turned out, I learned everything the hard way.

For the next fifteen years, I studied, travelled, and worked in American television doing everything opposite of how I was raised, terrified I would also die young. I made every choice as if it was the last choice of my life, which seems extreme but is, in fact, one of the best life hacks. Do it now. Be happy. Don't worry about what's coming because you can't control it anyway. Speak out. Be yourself. Don't let someone else's perception of you get in the way of how you want to live.

MY STYLE OF LEADING

Given the above, when faced with the challenge of leading the No More Lockdowns movement in Vancouver, I wondered okay, so what is *my* style of leadership? What is going to make me successful and impactful as a leader to help people understand they were being targeted and used in the greatest financial heist in the history of the world? How on earth was I going to accomplish that when the media, friends, family, and most of the province was, in fact, against me? How could I possibly lead people who didn't understand they even needed a leader? That was going to require magic, wonder, and sleight of hand – to show people something they didn't believe existed.

I looked back into the past three years of studying public health fraud in BC and assessed my ammunition ... sweet fuck all, really. A school PAC that thought I was a lunatic, family members who have no problem shaming me on social media for my beliefs, 80% less income than I had before Bonnie Henry opened her mouth on CTV, and two young kids who needed homeschooling, attention, and love from me. Not exactly an arsenal. *What did I have in abundance?* I wondered. What *was* available to me in spades? Anything? And then it hit me. What I had started doing one year earlier with an irreverent brand I designed – Health Justice – to help moms understand regulatory policy. *Mothers.* I had mothers, the most powerful weapon of all. As I learned in all my years of TV, mothers are *the most powerful force on the planet* because we control 80% of all household spending from cars to cable, flights to food. I put my TV commercial producer hat back on and hit Facebook to build an army.

Over the last twelve months of becoming one of Canada's key leaders exposing Covid fraud, many brutal and shocking experiences have befallen me. I won't dwell on them because the truth is these stories won't help mothers, who are my focus. What helps mothers most is education, emotional support, networking, and cold hard cash. All the things I watched my own mother create and take advantage of in her activism that helped to build up Vancouver's VanDuesen Botanical Gardens when I was a kid. This is always how women nurture and protect our families, how we build community, and how we lead – we do it together in simple, fast, cheap ways that work.

In case it helps, however, here is a short list of all the brutal battles I have had to fight to get my message out this year: I have been shamed by friends and extended family online; some of those relationships may never heal. My family has been evicted twice from rental homes, we lost 80% of our income, and my kids lost their right to education. I have been the victim of crimes under the Criminal Code of Canada, when the public has yelled at me, threatened me, and filmed me in private. I was violently and fraudulently fake-arrested by four sheriffs inside the BC Supreme Court and basically "abducted" into the basement for two hours to remove me from influencing a protest I didn't even know was going on. I have been lied about by the media, assaulted on a Vancouver bus, stalked by a mentally deranged man who sent me a sexually violent letter, and implicated on a WorkSafeBC fraudulent poster. Most recently, I was the victim of slander, defamation, and libel by a CTV Bell Canada Enterprises employee. I am now pursuing formal legal action with a small team of investors committed to media justice in Canada.

It's been nothing less than torture, really, but having twenty years of experience in activism, I am blessed with the wisdom to know none of the above was actually about me. It's about the truth and how it is silenced by the status quo in order to maintain it. The world I come from, the fringes of society I grew up on, and a few but incredibly corrupt people who take advantage of that society for their own personal financial gain. I am proud to share the stories of what I have endured but truthfully, I don't think

The Third Jeep

it helps people. I prefer to focus on solutions because that is where the big wins in human rights dwell.

The incredible lessons I learned during three intense months of leading the Vancouver protest marches April through June are many, but here are a few highlights. I learned that for social movements to succeed, strong inspiring leaders are absolutely required. People need leaders to show them the path, and it's a great opportunity for some of us who have those skills. Witnessing others be inspired by my passion and goals was thrilling, and I will always be humbled to have been given that unique opportunity. To lead hundreds of people through the streets of Vancouver where I grew up were some of the best moments of my life. The noise, the cheering, the joy, and the anger – every emotion the world was feeling was right behind me, pushing me forward to find new ways to get the truth out. Often it worked. It didn't always seem like it was working because to this day, the Vancouver and Canadian media refuse to tell the truth of Covid fraud, but our message was getting out there and people were hungry for the truth. We were changing the world, and we knew it. We were incredibly proud to be doing that.

After a few months of marches, I realized the war was not going to be won simply with marching. The media was our real enemy, which is why this book is so valuable. The war, still raging, is and will be won in the courts and in the court of public opinion. Only when enough people take back the authority to govern themselves they have so readily given away to the government will they ever be free again. I watch for that moment every single day as it grows slowly but surely around the world. I believe the people are truly awakening and rising up. They are learning the cruelest crimes are being committed by journalists who blatantly lie and manufacture fear because the shareholders who benefit from tyranny pay them to do so.

A NEW HEALTH ECONOMY

Because corruption is always and only about one thing – money, the opportunity that lies before those of us committed to natural health and human rights is nothing less than immense. Yes, immense. After twenty years of doing this work, I can promise you this: human rights are inextricably linked to the power of capital, economies, and the dignity and freedom those economies provide to those who inhabit them. That's just the way society works. Societies that create the most broad based wealth and health are the ones who also have the most personal freedoms.

Economists say that after fifty years and close to a trillion dollars of aid money shoveled into Africa, most of it was wasted. The single most powerful investment powering Africa today, making it one of the fastest growing economies in the world, is the SIM card. That tiny little piece of plastic inside your phone is giving Africans the opportunity to imagine and build the world they have always wanted for themselves. I believe that should be the focus for every one of us. How we can work in service to others and liberate the world from the growing tyranny we face? All of us have a role to play. Every effort counts even if you don't see results right away. You matter. Your voice does matter. Never ever lose sight of that. Justice for the many requires the effort of many, and the good people in the world far outweigh the bad. I believe this work is our next economy, what I call The Justice Economy.

WHY BRAVERY MATTERS

I am incredibly honoured to be included in this edition of *The Brave* and will summarize my story with the reasons why bravery matters. Without bravery, we go through our lives in fear, possibly never learning our true greatness and success because we are afraid to try. Without bravery, we become vulnerable to the tyranny and greed of others of which there is no limit; these bullies are everywhere. And without bravery, we lose one of the most important concepts in life – the idea that we need heroes to inspire us to believe we *can* live the lives we want in peace, happiness, and health.

I will finish with two of my favourite quotes by two of my biggest heroes who are brave beyond imagination:

"Every time we witness an injustice and do not act, we train our character to be passive in its presence and thereby eventually lose all ability to defend ourselves and those we love." – Julian Assange

"Be brave. Do something." – James O'Keefe

Every person matters. Every effort counts. Never be afraid to speak truth to power because if you don't challenge corruption, eventually you become a victim of it.

About Susan Standfield:

Growing up in Vancouver in the 1970s and '80s, Sue was raised to question society and work in service to others, values she hold close today at age fifty-two. Sue received a BA in Political Science from Queen's University at Kingston; she started her degree the same month she knew her mother had four months to live due to big tobacco and corrupt health policy in Canada. Looking back, that is the single most defining experience of her life. Sue has lived and worked all over the world, mostly in TV, design, and since 2001, in various roles of human rights work in Canada and Africa, where she calls home. In 2003 she founded her first social profit venture, moved to Africa in 2004, and after moving back to Vancouver in 2016, started the No More Lockdowns economic and natural health rights movement on April 12th, 2020, when she saw blatant and criminal evidence of organized public health fraud in British Columbia.

Susan has worked tirelessly speaking this truth to power for twelve straight months, paying a very high price for being a visible leader in a movement that has been worth every sacrifice to protect her children and all Canadian children from growing medical tyranny in Canada. Sue's work uses video and photo-based public pedagogy, educates women and moms about human rights vis-a-vis her brand Health Justice. Sue is one of those people who

The Third Jeep

ended up taking the road far less traveled at a young age because of failed health policy in Canada. It has made all the difference in creating a uniquely authentic life for her, her family, and a growing community of natural health activists she is proud to help lead.

HEALTH JUSTICE
With Susan Standfield
healthjusticetees.com
236 668 1009
healthjusticetees@gmail.com

Chapter Three

Canadian Frontline Nurse

By Kristen Nagle

London, Ontario has been my home for the past ten years. I worked as a nurse in the NICU at LHSC until my recent termination in January 2021. London has always held a special place in my heart. It is where I first moved away from home (Oakville, Ontario) at the age of nineteen to attend Western University for Nursing and earn my BScN.

I worked abroad and travelled across the globe for six years before meeting my husband and returning back to London to plant our roots. I have loved watching London's local businesses grow and thrive. I have always been an advocate for supporting local businesses and growing a community that is based on collaboration, not competition. My husband and I have loved attending festivals, organizing events, and meeting new people. I have always felt very connected to this city and those who also call it home. For this reason, it was sad to watch the people who knew me turn on me just because the media did.

When I became a mother, everything began to change for me. It has been said that our children are chosen for us, to show us what we truly want and need in our life. I fully believe this, as my firstborn reminded me of all of my passions that I seemed to have forgotten, and this reignited a fire inside of me.

When my son was born, I also realized it was my responsibility to decide what entered his body, knowing it would ultimately set the foundation for his future growth and development and impact his cells, behaviour, and mood. I wanted to be well-informed on such important decisions, so I attended the Canadian School of Natural Nutrition and became a Registered Holistic Nutritionist. This was a pivotal moment in my life. It went beyond learning about proper food for our children; it was the missing component I felt in nursing. Everything finally made sense to me. Conventional medicine was lacking an essential component to care, to life – it was the mind/body/spirit connection. I felt a burning desire, a passion to teach the world all that I was learning about food, holistic health, and our connection to the earth. I wanted to teach others how to create a healthy foundation for our children to grow and thrive, how to reconnect to ourselves, and understand our complex, divinely made bodies.

In 2016, Sweaty Successful Moms was founded by three mothers. We set out to create a community that believes in raising leaders who are wholeheartedly connected to the earth. Our mission has been to empower women to live their lives with passion and purpose, allowing them to then teach their children to lead with their hearts and change the world. We didn't realize at the time how important this message would be in the coming years and how much it would shape the stance I would personally take, fully stepping into my purpose and leading.

It has always been a running joke in my family that as a child I could not lie. I was even told it would be easier if I would just suck up to my teachers. The truth of how I was feeling was always painted on my face for all to see. There was no denying how I truly felt about something. I have always held strong to my beliefs and would call out untruth when I came across it.

I don't think my parents realize the impact they have had on me to be able to find my voice and to develop the courage to speak up for the truth. My dad has always been my hero. A retired chief, firefighter of thirty-seven years in Toronto, he was the epitome of integrity, strength, and compassion. He always maintained his values while still extending mutual respect and understanding to others he may not agree with. This is what earned him the respect of many in his life because he always listened to others with patience and never judged them.

My mom is one of the most amazing women I know. Her words have always been honest even if, at times, they were hard to hear. She has always spoken the truth, and nothing is sugar-coated. She would consistently see through any deception and challenge it. Her unconditional love supported me throughout my life, even through difficult times. Her compassion and willingness to help those in need never went unnoticed. I don't think to this day she realizes how strong of a role model she has been for me.

Although the truth was painted on my face and I had strong beliefs, throughout my adolescence I struggled with wanting to feel accepted and to fit in. I would try to shape myself into the person I thought would be more liked. I was an academic, but I longed to be invited to the cool kids' parties. I drank and partied excessively and made terrible decisions with boys in my life. I ended up in situations that left me feeling empty, alone, and unworthy of love. It wasn't until recently, when I reflected on this time in my life, that I saw how much I tried to change who I was to fit into a place where I never belonged and that was never meant for me. The last five years of my life I have been on a path to being truly, unabashedly me. Thankfully my husband has always seen and loved the true me and has been a huge source of support throughout this journey, especially now in my new role as an advocate.

2020 was the year I stepped into fully being the person I was always destined to become with no regrets. Yet, I still feared imposter syndrome. Who am I to be speaking on such topics? I don't know enough, and I'm not educated enough. I was just an ordinary person, a mom who said enough is enough. This was the year that pushed me to all my limits, to stand with purpose and passion, and to go against the grain. I decided to not fit in, to be rejected, and to stand in my power and truth. It is the year that has been the most freeing for me.

I have been vocal on social media about true health and well-being for several years now. I have spoken about health being found from within rather than from injections or pills. When news of the virus in Wuhan hit the mainstream, I knew immediately that the truth was not being told. I tried with increased urgency to educate everyone I could on the importance of health created within us. It was met with a lot of backlash. My voice became louder as the lockdowns began in March of 2020, and I understood the agenda behind all of it. I was labelled a conspiracy theorist, anti-science, reckless, and dangerous. I was shunned by family and friends, and, of course, colleagues. I didn't stop. I knew what was at stake, and I no longer feared rejection. Our freedoms, life as we knew it, sovereignty over our bodies, and our ability to choose against mandated vaccinations were all being destroyed at record speed. The stage was being set for the Great Reset and Agenda 2030 – seventeen sustainable development goals that sound great on paper but are gravely detrimental to society around the globe.

I had an opportunity to speak at city hall regarding masks on children in September of 2020. It was time that I took action in person for the words I had been sharing on social media. I went to speak after a night shift with little sleep and poured my heart out. The video ended up going viral, which led to meeting more advocates who have been fighting for our children. This empowered me to keep going, even with the steady backlash, including being suspended from work. A friend and I decided it was time to truly take a stance in London and host a freedom rally under Sweaty Successful Moms on November 22nd, 2020. The event was a huge success, and we felt so proud of what we had accomplished in our hometown. The media picked up on it immediately, and this was the first time my name would be slandered publicly across mainstream media in Canada. I was then suspended indefinitely from work and placed under investigation by the College of Nurses of Ontario. We were also charged on two counts for hosting the rally and attending the rally (upon writing this chapter, no actual court date has happened yet for these charges).

I was prepared for a lot of backlash, but I was not prepared for the public humiliation brought to my name that labelled me as irresponsible. They inferred that I was putting premature babies at risk. My entire nursing career was defamed, and I was labeled as a bad nurse. This hurt me to my core because it was so far from the truth. Every moment, hour, and day I worked, I have always carried each baby in my heart. I loved them wholeheartedly and have cherished the relationships I developed with their families. I was speaking out to protect them and their future. I spent many nights crumpled on the floor, sobbing, laying in my tears, and crying myself to sleep. When you are reported to the College, you are able to read every report made about you, this included local businesses and even one from a family member. I felt the pain, the hurt, the anger, the betrayal, and the sadness. All of it. I let it flow through me and fuel me. I would not let it break me, and when I was ready, I picked myself up off the floor and put the pieces back together stronger than before. I wasn't going to quit or be silenced.

This led to finding other nurses speaking out, such as Sarah Choujounian. in Toronto. Together, we founded Canadian Frontline Nurses and flew to DC to speak with other American nurses with the Global Frontline Nurses on a health and freedom stage. It was so empowering to be united with other nurses who shared the same concerns.

Upon our return to Canada, we were met with more media slander and defamation. This time, it was on an international level. We were labeled domestic terrorists by the media and as a result, we both had the RCMP show up at our door. All for trying to speak the truth about what was happening, and for advocating for the health and well-being of patients and our communities. We were also officially and publicly terminated from our employment.

This time it wouldn't break me, and I was ready. Every attempt they made to silence me, my voice only grew louder and with more confidence and conviction. I was here, and I was standing firm. Every step I have taken, I have led with my heart, following the truth and my intuition. It has led me to connecting with some of the most amazing people I know. Through the Canadian Frontline Nurses, we have connected with so many nurses all across Canada who feel the same way as we do. Sarah and I together have travelled to BC to speak to crowds that filled our hearts with love and support. Many speaking engagements, interviews, and opportunities continue to present themselves. For someone that once feared rejection and standing out, I have never felt more alive, more confident, and more like me than in any other time of my life.

The gift that 2020 has given to us, if we choose to accept it, is to fully and unapologetically embrace who we truly are in life. We can begin chipping away anything that is not aligned with our hearts and stepping into the greatness that we are uniquely made for, with our own magic to share. This greatness is built by taking one ordinary, brave step at a time toward the person we want to be and the future we wish to have. From this perspective, the year that was meant to destroy us all is, in fact, the most special gift we could have been given in life.

There's a quote that continues to inspire and lead me: "The price for standing up for Truth, no matter how severe, will always be less than the price our souls will be penalized for not speaking up for our conscience. There is no greater crime in the universe than silencing your conscience." - Suzy Kassem.

For me there was no other option. Staying quiet was only hurting my soul, and I did not see an alternative. I have no idea what is next after all of this, but I know I am protected and I am safe. I will continue to fight for truth for my young boys and all of the children out there. I will continue to stand firm in truth against all adversity. I have to be able to look back and know I stood for something. I want my boys to know I fought for them.

Faith has also been an essential component to speaking out and what continues to give me immense strength and hope. Whatever your faith may be, hold onto it firmly and let it ground you and strengthen you. I know at this time in history that those who are standing up and speaking the truth are standing on the right side of it.

This is a movement of ordinary citizens taking extraordinary steps of bravery. Each small act of bravery you take is an essential part of the change that is taking place. Take some time to consider all of the small and big ways that you can take action in your own life.

We still have challenges to come, but I am so excited for what we are all capable of creating. The systems need to collapse for us to come in and create something beautiful. Keep your frequencies high, raise your vibrations, and stay focused on the future you want for yourself and for future generations. Continue to hold onto that, because it is what we are working toward now. That is what we are all going to create together.

About Kristen Nagle:

Kristen Nagle had been a nurse for fourteen years, primarily in the neonatal intensive care unit before being terminated in January 2021 for speaking up against the narrative. When Kristen's first son was born, she realized the importance food would have in creating the foundation for his growth and development and enrolled at the Canadian School of Natural Nutrition. She also became a holistic nutritionist in 2018. As a holistic nutritionist, Kristen is able to understand both conventional medicine as well as a more holistic approach that incorporates the mind, body, and spirit to uncover the root cause of illness. This led to further research into iatrogenic disease, vaccines, and pharmaceutical propaganda. It was through this education that Kristen was able to have a deeper understanding of true health and well-being and see through the media perpetuated fear that surrounded the "pandemic." Kristen believes in medical transparency and informed consent, which is currently lacking in the health care system. Kristen has witnessed unethical measures as a neonatal nurse which has empowered her to speak up and advocate for the babies who do not yet have a voice. Her first speaking debut was at her local city hall regarding masks on school children. This led her to speaking at other freedom rallies, eventually organizing her own successful freedom march in her hometown.

Kristen is passionate about children's health and empowering families to trust their bodies and immune systems, to support and not suppress symptoms, and to live a more natural life in harmony with the earth with full body sovereignty.

www.CanadianFrontlineNurses.com

Chapter Four

Fearless

By Alicia Christine Johnson

To be selfish is easy. To be selfless takes sacrifice.

I have always lived by these words which I wrote many years ago. I've lived a life faced with many instances of adversity. I was a child subjected to many things that no child should see, hear, or experience. I grew up witnessing alcoholism, drug addiction, physical, mental, verbal abuse, and manipulation. Sadly, I was never protected from these things. It forced me to grow up as an adult trapped in a child's body, having to learn how to shield and protect myself.

Despite all these things I endured, I truly believe I was given a gift. That gift was the ability to watch what was happening around me and learn from it, thus making me who I am today. When I see what is going on in the world right now, it is affirmation as to why I was put in all those environments.

It was teaching me discernment.

I have always been a strong voice against all costs, standing up for what is right rather than following what is popular. There is something inside me that innately wants to protect those who cannot protect themselves — maybe it's because that was not done for me. I became a mother very young; I was nineteen years old when I had my daughter. I knew when I first held her that I would do everything in my power to give her the life I never had and the childhood I never got to experience.

When this manufactured pandemic was executed onto the world, my instinct to fight, to protect my daughter's future and those who could not see what this was, ran through me like a firestorm.

I remember standing in my kitchen after Justin Trudeau announced they were going to shut down the country for two weeks to brace for what's to come. In that very moment, my stomach churned like a hand was grabbing my insides and twisting them into a knot. My instincts were telling me this was not genuine, that this was not the truth. And as time passed, everything from that moment was like watching a chess game, foreseeing every move they were going to make before they made it.

I have done many things over the past twenty years "career" wise. Reflecting more and more on those vast areas of work, I realized they were all to give me the skills I needed to recognize the fraud we were seeing with COVID-19.

I currently live in Vancouver, British Columbia, Canada and have an agency in the wholesale industry for gift and souvenir retail. Many of the suppliers I work with get their products manufactured directly in China, and that was the first tip-off for me. As Canada and the entire western world was shutting down, China was up, running, and manufacturing again. If this was a genuine pandemic, what I saw on mainstream media — people dropping dead, laying in the streets – was not logically possible. The videography we saw was propaganda and not authentic. There are over 1.4 billion people who reside in China. If there was a deadly and highly contagious pathogen, it is impossible for a country that has more than thirty-six times the population of Canada to completely recover, return to manufacturing goods, and living their life freely as they have been since March 2020.

Before building my agency in the wholesale sector, I worked very closely with surgeons, anesthesiologists, nurses, and sterile technicians in the private surgical sector. I was blessed with experience in the medical/surgical arena. My employer, a plastic surgeon, was a very hands-on teacher and invited me to scrub in for surgeries so that I could observe and learn about each procedure, as well as learn the protocols for each surgical staff member as we ran two operating rooms. Because of this, I am very versed in areas of sterile environments, protocols, and surgical masks. This was yet another trigger for me, knowing that masks do not assist in protecting you against viral infections, yet the public health officers and officials around the world were blatantly lying to the public telling them it was a measure of protection.

I am also fortunate to have a mother who is a long-term care nurse. I grew up learning how politics superseded the care of our elderly in these homes. There would be days my mother would come home angry and crying out of sheer frustration because of the lack of care and concern for her patients by the administration and the government. Her patients would be fed overcooked/boiled or liquefied food with zero nutrition. The staff even started taking away the little things that gave her patients some joy and comfort, like tea and cookies. My mother would take it upon herself to bring those little things in for her patients because they deserved better.

The government has never cared about our elderly. When I heard the government say they are working so hard to convince the public that this was the only way to protect the elderly, I knew it was a blatant lie. This was just a calculated manipulation to coerce people into doing what they needed them to do by lying to the public and using people's emotions against them without them realizing it.

Our elderly in long-term care are the perfect scapegoat to execute such a grand manipulation, knowing how many die annually in long term care every flu season. It was the perfect scenario for the government because they know the general public is not aware of how many pass away during this time. Not only from viral flu but also after being given the flu vaccine because their bodies and immune systems are so weak, they can't recover from it. The key here is that no one has ever shone a light on our long-term care facilities until now. The horrifying truth is that people are witnessing this, and it has been happening for decades. But the only ones who know of these facts are the long-term care staff who are bound by confidentiality agreements and cannot speak out without losing their jobs.

This is when I knew this was going to be a very serious fight. The biggest fight I had ever taken on.

Fighting the government and the propaganda machine felt like David and Goliath. But I know in the end, good always wins and the truth will always prevail. That has shown itself to me my entire life, and in that I trust.

I started paying very close attention to all data and statistics, pulling up everything I could to start showing people that this was medical fraud. My business shut down completely when they locked the world down and, looking back, I couldn't be more grateful. It gave me every hour of every day to research as much as I could to uncover every piece of information and evidence I could find to figure out what their plan was. There were many days I would get four hours of sleep per night if I was lucky. I have always been when something is not right, I will do whatever it takes to make sure people cannot get away with hurting others. I am relentless; I do not and will not give up. This isn't the first time I have gone up against people who have ill intentions for others. But when I know something is catastrophically wrong and needs to be exposed, I will do everything in my power and will not rest until what's been done is undone.

When I started exposing all the evidence of fraud I found — patents, legal documents, medical scientific literature, science and medical professionals speaking out – people immediately started to chastise me with all sorts of defamatory slanderous names. Fortunately for me, I've been through enough in my life, and I have very thick skin in that regard. I knew it would only be a matter of "when" I could start turning some of those people around. Liars can never keep their lie straight, and I knew it was only a matter of time.

I had family walk away from me as well. They believed what they were being told despite all the evidence I shared with them. Although knowing my career experience and the education I've received during that time, they disregarded me and behaved in very poor taste, throwing insults and being dismissive. Sadly, still to this day, I have people who were very close to me that now have little to do with me because they refuse to acknowledge any information that is given to them that doesn't come from the mainstream media. But I still carry on in hopes they will eventually see what's being done, not only to themselves, but to those they've been convinced they are protecting, and the atrocity that is being committed to our children and humanity as a whole.

Mother's Day was the first COVID-19 lockdown protest I attended, where I met like-minded people who knew this was a fraud. I knew participating so openly would place my business at risk, but I knew there would be no future for business if we let the government carry out its plans for humanity. I went in full force, trusting that whatever happens, everything will work out, no matter how it unfolded.

I began going to every rally that was held in Vancouver, BC. I began to speak openly to my clients and my suppliers, not fearing repercussion because I knew the alternative was far worse. I opened all my social media platforms and set them to public view so people could see the content I was sharing. From there, the advocacy work I was doing started to grow vastly.

I met other leaders here in Vancouver and across Canada who were advocating the same truth I was. We began to collaborate, with some of us becoming very tightly knit, doing our own advocacy separately and then coming together as a community. From that community the freedom movement, Freedom Rally World and The Freedom Organization, was born. We host the largest Freedom Rallies in British Columbia bringing in doctors, scientists, virologists, microbiologists, nurses, and other speakers from around the world who the government, mainstream media, and Big Tech try to censor. Our goal is to help educate people and expose the truth. The newly birthed "The Freedom Organization" is the largest virtual platform for our Freedom for Truth Conferences. We aid in educating as many people as possible in Canada and around the world and give a voice to those with disabilities or those in fear of repercussion. We are a community that exists to strengthen their voices. We have had over 20,000 people join in less than thirty days, many of them doctors, nurses, firefighters, teachers, and police officers.

The only way we get out of this is through knowledge and teaching people the truth. Showing them what they are not being told.

What some don't yet realize is the long game of this government and many other governments around the world. So many people believe they are going to get their lives back with a vaccine. What they don't understand is that COVID-19 is the gateway to convincing the world to kneel to a false sense of security. While doing so, you relinquish freedom and bodily sovereignty to a governance that has only ever wanted more control, not less.

Myself and many others like me will not allow this to happen. We will fight for those who cannot fight: our elderly, our children, and for all those who have not yet realized what this is really about – human enslavement and no longer being free.

I have always been fearless when standing in the face of adversity. When you walk without fear and you lead with conviction, knowing that what you fight for is right, there is nothing more powerful than standing for the truth. Being fearless never comes easy, but the only way to hold your own power is by facing fear.

This Ends when We Stand.

About Alicia Christine Johnson:

Alicia Johnson was born in Victoria, British Columbia, Canada. She studied Business Technology at Kwantlen University. She is a mother and sister of five younger siblings. Alicia has worked in the music-industry, events industry, tourism industry, medical/surgical industry, and is now an entrepreneur with her own agency in wholesale goods and-service-in-the-retail/souvenir sector. Her passion has always been humanitarian work, music, and the arts. She is the co-founder of Freedom Rally World and The Freedom Organization, two advocacy institutions that share knowledge for human rights and medical freedom from the tyranny we are seeing today in global governments and pharmaceutical institutions. Alicia has always been a voice of strength for those who cannot speak up or stand up for themselves.

To find Alicia on social media, please go to:
Instagram: @aliciacj
Twitter: aliciajohnson_
Telegram: https://t.me/AliciaJohnson777
Facebook: www.facebook.com/aliciajohnson7777777
The Freedom Org: www.thefreedomorg.ca
IG:The Freedom Org
Twitter: @TheFreedomOrg_
Freedom Rally World: www.freedomrally.world
IG: FreedomRally.World
Twitter: @FreeRallyWorld

Chapter Five

A Mom's Legacy

By Kimberly Nuedorf

I'm Kimberly.

I'm a wife and stay-at-home homeschool mom. I've traveled a bit, but for now I've ended up back where I started – in a farming community in southwestern Ontario, namely Aylmer.

A long time ago, I got my BMus in performance (flute) at the University of Western Ontario in London. Then I got married, had three children, and here I am!

My life has been pretty uneventful until 2020. I organized and ran two fantastic freedom marches in my hometown, one in October and one in November. For that effort I received four summonses from police to appear in a St. Thomas court to face four charges – two for attending and two for organizing the marches. I later received a fifth summons to appear in a London court to face a similar charge after speaking at the Freedom Rally in London, Ontario in November of 2020.

When it comes to protecting freedoms, everyone has a part to play. This is the part that I can play. Standing for our freedom to keep encroaching government at bay, so I can continue to provide a healthy environment and a world full of opportunity for my children to grow up in is my most important effort – my legacy.

A Mom's Legacy

Some days I ask myself, "How did I get here?"

This is why I'm here.

There was a distinct moment in my life that I now see as a defining event. It was an innocent question from an old friend who just had a baby. She was mentioning all the decisions she needed to make as a new mother, one of which included the decision about vaccinations. She asked me, "What will you choose?" I remember being completely startled and thought to myself, "I have a choice?"

In that moment I realized I had responsibility over my life and my path and that of my children. With this sudden realization, I decided I had sure better equip myself with the information I needed to take on that huge responsibility. Since then, I've always advocated for my family and for the choices we decide are the best for us in order to live our best lives. I decided not to delegate the responsibility of the well-being of my family to the state. This applies to all areas of my family's life, including education and healthcare.

Is that bravery? Maybe. Brave in the fact that if something goes wrong or isn't ideal, that would be on me. Taking responsibility means I can't place the blame on a doctor or a teacher or a system if something doesn't go well, but it also means I can be so proud when it goes right! It's the way families ought to navigate through life. A mother has an intuition of what is best for their own child and what they need to thrive. No agency or system will ever get that right.

Already in my early twenties, before children, I was an outspoken advocate for natural health and food. In 2020, when government overreach started crossing some of the lines that we had long established in our family, I felt it necessary to become much more outspoken about the loss of these freedoms and responsibilities, and the infringement on the family to make their own choices.

The word *opportunity* has resonated with me from day one of this false pandemic. Opportunity is very closely tied to liberty, and an incredibly important aspect that government overreach has robbed from us is opportunity. Whether or not I choose to participate in all of the opportunities available to me in this world is not the issue here – the opportunities must be there. I have a close friend who lives quite hermit-like but has become quite depressed during these restrictions because the world is not turning as it should. The opportunities, however little he partook of them, have been taken away from him and that is a depressing life. He sees those that he loves being robbed of their opportunities. In light of all the accusations of selfishness I've encountered, I can't think of a more selfless attitude than my friend's. Life goes on, and we *care deeply* that life must go on, not just for ourselves but for everyone.

Living is inherently risky. We are not robots; we are humans with emotion and intelligence beyond programming. We constantly evaluate the risks because everything has a trade-off. There's nuance in taking those daily risks, and that's on us. There's no way that broad overarching public policy can in any way take into account those nuances, and it's the height of folly to allow those risks to be taken out of our hands.

I'm often asked why I defied the law in running two freedom marches. In fact, I was following the law. This was actually *not* civil disobedience. No judge has ruled that freedoms, as defined in the Charter, have been suspended during COVID-19. My actions cannot be labeled civil disobedience until judges have ruled that the Charter has been suspended, and to this point they have not done so and seem afraid to do so, postponing trials including mine. It is absolutely necessary that these cases get to the courts; this has to happen so we know where we stand. What does the Charter actually mean anymore? Are we indeed a free country or not? I'm banking on the fact that we are still a free country, and the courts will rule accordingly. If I'm wrong, I will pay a price for my decisions. If we're not a free country, we certainly should be alarmed. I'm standing up for my free country. I am standing up for children, families, the vulnerable, and for life in this country as we know it.

Early during the first lockdown in 2020, we took our children to play in boarded-up or taped-off parks. It may seem like a small act, but as I've often found out, small acts of courage lead to further acts of courage. I'm doing nothing differently in running the freedom marches than I have done for all the previous years of motherhood. Those years have meant providing opportunities and a vibrant environment for my children to thrive. Now I need to protect those opportunities from disappearing. Incredibly, running those freedom marches led to five charges that carry a maximum fine of $500,000 and up to five years in prison if convicted.

I was inspired by a few other moms who had organized Freedom Rallies throughout the year, so finally in October 2020 I organized my first rally. I researched how to have a lawful public march, followed all of the necessary steps for that, and put out social media posts quite last minute. With just over twenty-four hours' notice in a small town of 7,500 people, the word spread quickly and we had 300 enthusiastic people turn out. It was very successful, and people were so thankful and encouraged by the gathering.

We decided to have another one two weeks later. Before it was even planned, there was a lot of media furor and attention, and many interviews were requested. Many of them wanted an answer as to why the rallies were necessary. To even ask that question seemed to me an indication that people had no understanding of what the role of peaceful protest, and even civil disobedience, plays in a healthy, free society. The rallies were the uniting of the voices of families speaking against how governments have handled COVID-19 so incredibly poorly, that what is called for goes way beyond some kind of *flouting of public health regulations*. It calls for a strong challenge to the conditions and decrees under which people would flout public health regulations in the first place.

The amount of people who responded to the rallies with "it's just a piece of cloth" or "wouldn't you wear your seatbelt" is the type of low-resolution thinking that has obviously allowed governments to trample all over our liberties in the first place. It takes deep, philosophical, careful, multi-layered thinking to address complex issues like Covid-19, and that is evidently lacking not only among most people, but sadly among those who are sworn to protect our individual liberty. Many people expressed that the rally gave them great encouragement, that it was the first time they realized they weren't alone in their thinking, and that there were many like-minded people willing to stand up against these tyrannical measures. Courage is far more infectious than any virus.

I announced our second freedom rally for November 7th with a little more notice, and the same meticulous details given to the police about the route, timing, and scope of the event. Hilariously, our town council declared a state of emergency. They went even further beyond the pale in threatening to charge everyone in attendance not wearing masks but were apparently reminded by the police that the health orders included exemptions from mask-wearing for about half a dozen categories (health, creed, ability, etc.) Rather than stopping there, our town's mayor (of 7,500 people) outdid herself in the *chutzpah* category by calling on the Solicitor General of Ontario to rescind the mask exemptions so as to allow for large-scale charges to be laid. Of course, the council labelled our marches as "anti-mask rallies" – a rallying cry that was picked up by most media outlets. The media attention, which had largely been missing from large rallies and marches in large cities, was intense. Our second march started trending on Twitter, and the positive result of the negative publicity was that more and more people heard of our freedom march and made plans to attend. I suppose in retrospect I should have sent flowers of gratitude to the mayor.

I started hearing of groups from far and wide planning to attend, and counter-protesters started agitating for a large-scale response, including threats of violence. There were moments where it became a little overwhelming, and for a few intense days we contemplated whether it might be wise to cancel or postpone our family-friendly freedom march. But as there seemed no good reason to allow the threat of counter-protest to succeed in thwarting us, and since we had already proven to be completely peaceful, I forged ahead. There was a lot of stress in the days preceding the event – a lot of police visits, a lot of unnecessary measures, and a lot of intimidation by the town, who clearly were way out of their depth in their study of the Charter *specifically*, and democracy *generally*. I suppose we shouldn't have been surprised.

In the end, it was an overwhelming success. Police estimates pegged attendance at *2,000 people. In a town of 7,500.* There was elation and much relief that apart from a few scuffles, the event was peaceful and proactive. The speakers brought important information to bear on the situation. Even now, after what seems like a lifetime since the marches, I am constantly thankful that constitutional lawyer Rocco Galati (by way of a weekly zoom meeting with Vaccine Choice Canada) decided to represent me *pro bono,* and also supported me by writing letters to the town and the local police. To the town, he wrote about the unconscionable declaration of a state of emergency, "an abuse of power and authority." To the police, he wrote about the recorded intimidation tactics that grew increasingly heavy-handed the closer we got to November 7th. He continues to represent and support me for as long as is necessary to see these charges through and has done so for numerous other clients. When we look back on Canadian history of 2020-21, I have no doubt that Rocco's name will be in the history books for the right reasons.

There have been court dates. To date, they've all been postponed. People have often asked me if I'm afraid. After our house was visited on three separate occasions in the dead of the night, with furious pounding on our doors and windows, I was unsettled. But I'm not afraid. There are times where I have fear, but foundationally I am not afraid - I decided not to be. *Fear Not!* is a phrase spoken some fifty plus times by Jesus as recorded in the scriptures, and I take that exhortation seriously. If you look around, the world is still alive. The birds are still chirping; the sun still rises and sets.

A Mom's Legacy

When life is confusing, you don't make decisions out of fear. If you don't know the way to go, you go toward freedom. That's what God wants for us - He always moves people toward freedom. Ultimately people have always been willing to pay the highest costs for the ideal of freedom. People don't send their young men to war for lowly ideals. They are willing to sacrifice everything for that singular ideal – freedom. At the same time, I'm not naïve to the fact that freedom won't eliminate death or illness and difficulties. That's life! But neither does the cult of *COVID-19ism.* Freedom simply draws us together in those difficulties to serve one another and be part of each other's lives. I live by the ideal that we cannot and should not try to control other people's lives, and that *life is only life* when there are trials and triumphs.

If I am honest with myself, I've had no choice but to do what I've done. It's my job as a mother, a neighbour, and a human. I'm doing what I *can* do. Other people have other talents, ideas, and skills that they can bring to the battle for liberty, but I can hold rallies, encourage people to connect, help moms like me take on more responsibility for their families, and grow a network of free people. It's so important to me to play the lead part in my own life. God has given me the faculties to think and has given me the responsibility of serving Him with those faculties. Some people will leave a legacy of great wealth and influence. That probably won't be mine, but my aim has always been to pass along *this* legacy as a mother and a fellow human.

"Liberty, Sancho, my friend, is one of the most precious gifts that Heaven has bestowed on mankind." - Don Quixote.

About Kimberly Nuedorf:

Kimberly has been married to Terry since her university days and is a stay-at-home homeschool mom to Louisa, Oliver, and Sophie. She has enjoyed doing many creative things with her family, including performing together as the band, Vogel Joy. Later, her children acted professionally in numerous theater productions including *Macbeth* (Stratford Festival) and the Hallmark movie *Christmas Connection*. Her philosophy of education is influenced greatly by the Charlotte Mason method. In 2020, she took the plunge with her high school aged children, abandoning the accredited public education coursework and adopting the Ron Paul Curriculum. Kimberly enjoys researching and learning about natural health, functional patterns in movement, biohacking, and epigenetics. Currently she faces five charges under the Reopening Ontario Act for running two freedom rallies in her hometown of Aylmer, Ontario, and for speaking at another in London, Ontario. She continues to fight and strive for an abundant, free, fulfilling world for her children to grow up in.

www.kimberlyneudorf.com

Chapter Six

To Be Brave

By Jodi Lynn

I am going to start by saying this chapter will not be like any of the rest. In fact, I questioned Lani if I was a good fit for this book, as I was not sure if the readers would be ready for my story. It is quite unique and "out there" in many respects. However, my experiences, sacrifices, and contributions around Covid hold merit and quality and are very distinctive to me and what I do. To this day, it continues to mold and shape me to my highest calling and timeline, and I gladly answer the call. For this reason, I have been asked to share my past, my growth, and the paths I took of courage and bravery to help usher in and assist this monumental "shift" Covid is helping our world birth.

To help give clarity, I first need to take you back a bit to help you understand my history and who I was prior to 2020.

I was born in Surrey, BC and raised in a strict home of Jehovah's Witnesses. I was married at nineteen only to leave my husband and religion behind at twenty, after I met who would be my next husband. My choice to leave came at a very dear price and resulted in what the JW's refer to as being "disfellowshipped." This means you are disowned from your friends and family, as well as everyone practicing the religion. You are not welcome back until you repent, comply, and "fall back in line." Although I found a wonderful man to spend the next twenty years of my life with, I was tormented with spiritual guilt, personal inadequacies, and turbulent emotional rollercoasters.

This is when my journey of self-discovery and spiritual awakening really began. Looking back, through my "Covid goggles," I realize this was when my training and preparation for what I do now really started. It laid my foundation and instilled skills for what I was going to be asked to do in 2020 to assist mankind through this slippery and monumental transition.

Since I was little, my parents will attest, I always had a defiant attitude, so when I did not comply and come back to the JW religion, this disobedience came with swift and harsh consequences. I was being forced to believe a certain way, act accordingly, or be kicked out and ostracized unless I complied with the "rules." That never did resonate with me, nor would it ever! I craved the thought of a newfound freedom, and it stirred something deep inside to find what the "truth" really was, to find a way of being that resonated more with my body and the ways of my heart.

This would prove easier said than done. The next twenty years of my life were riddled with painful medical and emotional flare ups as I fought and fumbled my way to understanding these hidden truths. I attracted a car accident, sympathetic dystrophy (a mental phenomenon that paralyzed my entire leg), alopecia areata (I lost half of my hair), and most recently, an autoimmune disorder where my entire body swelled up and itched profusely for four months. These lessons taught me that when I ignored, numbed, or had any pity parties around my pain, it would often reappear and even get worse! That the location of where the pain manifested in my body would tell me what it was pertaining or relating to the most. Heart issues are around giving and receiving love; throat issues are around speaking your truth and how you express yourself and your emotions. As a result, I quickly realized that if I did not deal with my emotional pain and the shadow work (healing of past traumas), my body was going to make sure I did, and it was going to be much harder than it had to be.

For these reasons, I began down the path of holistics and spirituality as I realized these were missing elements in my life and very much went hand in hand. I learned reiki, meditation, as well as different forms of healing modalities. I learned about the importance of crystals, oils, and took courses to learn mediumship and angel card readings. Realizing my love and gift for what I was learning, I opened my All Things Healing business and began teaching many courses and offering my healing services. Courses included learning how to ascend from 3D to 5D, healing your inner child and sacred wounds (aka "shadow work"), as well as how to ground, shield, and clear your energy. Many of these teachings were channeled and divinely inspired. Techniques to help with the emotional healing process so it's not so violent. Rather, it's intentional, mindful and you manage the present moment rather than reacting to your emotions as you bounce back and forth from the past to the future. Master weapons and superpower tools that are more pertinent to learn now than ever.

In August of 2016, I began to feel the winds of change and a pull from my "spiritual team," so I chose to be brave again and found the courage to leave my last husband. I did not love him the way I should have, and I could feel the call of a new chapter unfolding for myself. So, I packed up and drove over 1200 km to a small town just outside of Fort St. John in northern BC. I only knew one social friend, so I had a lot of alone time. I spent the next four years learning to rely heavily on my connection with my spiritual team as I once again tried to get clear on my purpose and what I wanted in life. It was ever changing and very unclear at the time.

I was in a failing bad boy-type relationship as I attempted to defy what I never got to experience when I was younger. Although fun, it left me wanting more; I was unsatisfied and emotionally drained. This is where I found myself coming into 2020, and this is the part of my story where it gets interesting and all my life dots begin to connect. I say this because I did not require the kind of "brave" that was asked of most of the authors in this book. I did not take on restrictions or regulations that were imposed upon us during the pandemic. I did not even protest or defy many of the orders during this time. In fact, until recently, I even wore a mask. My bravery required courage of a different kind, a different realm!

During the spring and summer of 2020, I noticed myself changing a lot, especially in respect to my job, love life, and more importantly, my spiritual connection. It was becoming increasingly harder to go to work, and I had no drive and little energy most of this time. Then, my meditations started going to a whole other level. I began seeing Galactics come to visit and heal me, such as the Pleadians and Arcturians. I would watch with my third eye as they would lay their hands on me and remove "technology," as they called it, from my body – implants that needed to be removed. Often this tall being would enter during my reiki meditations. He had a large head that got smaller and flatter at the back and wore a long dark silky gown that went to the floor. He would intricately work on my solar area, sometimes working on one implant for many sessions with me. "He," due to his male energy I felt, would ask me to breathe in a specific way, and I would see upon my exhale items being removed as we worked together on my healings.

That is when the attacks began. Spiritual attacks by demons and dark entities. This was very new to me but extremely integral to learn so I could protect myself from what was about to be asked of me moving forward.

Once during a meditation, I had a three-headed being in a black robe with red lining came at me snarling and growling, its faces distorting the closer it got to me. Suddenly, an older man with a perfect beard walked in, grabbed it by the back of the neck, and cast it away with might. This is when I was guided to protect myself more and to surround myself with their love, protection, and light to keep me safe from any eye that wished me harm. I wore crystals, oils, and even was guided to set up crystal grids when I slept, as they said I was being attacked during my sleep. The dark was seeing my light, and this was their attempt to dim it.

They guided me, and I listened and trusted. This is when I took my next big leap of courage in October of 2020, when I asked my team to take me to the next level and use me for the greater good. I had no family obligations or attachments, a dying relationship I was preparing to leave, and a burning desire to help this world transcend to its next evolutionary level. I remember lying there in meditation, tears rolling down my face, surrounded by

Angelic and Galactic Beings, asking them to let me serve them. I remembered many lives here on Earth, and I knew what my mission was here this time - I was letting them know that. I was asking them to "take me" as it were. I had done the work, learned so many skills and life lessons, and if I could help mankind in this most crucial stage of ascension, I was offering myself. Whatever they needed of me, I promised them I would show up. I was completely illuminated in euphoric white light, and they asked me if I was ready and knew what that entailed. That there was a "process," and I knew that to mean a purging. A letting go, a releasing of old patterns and beliefs to make way for the new, and to this I agreed. And purging it was! On so many levels.

My autoimmune was triggered, and my eczema flared to encompass all my arms and legs with a severe rash. They were badly swollen and itched at a constant state of torture. My skin oozed and released what felt, and looked like, a lifetime of chemicals, toxins, and 3D residue. My team increased their healings on me, and often this was my only time of peace. They would knock me out so I could sleep, as it was nearly impossible to do so otherwise with the pain. Month after month it got worse and worse, and it was during this time I was attacked again and again by dark forces. Demons hurling energy at me to weaken me even further. I could feel and see their attacks, and with desperate tears I would yell at them "Is that all you got?" Then there were times I would beg my team to turn the pain down because it was almost unbearable, and they would whisper, "We already are." I knew I had to push through; this was my battle to endure and win, and win I would. I knew it was a test, and I was not going to let them win. I was too close. Not now.

To Be Brave

My team then asked me to use my body to channel much needed light energy into the world, to which I gladly agreed. This would be done by different colors being drawn through my crown and body to exit my hands but primarily my feet. I would do this often, lying down and allowing my body to be used as a beam of light for whatever energy needed to come in. The color they used the most was gold. Then, my team asked more of me and showed me they needed to channel energy out of the world. I agreed and began to see a slow stream of dark light begin to enter my solar area and exit out though my throat. It was like it needed my body as a conduit to channel the energy out, and the more I trusted and allowed this flow to happen, the quicker and thicker the stream became. I could feel this energy was heavy and dark but felt safe knowing Archangel Michael was protecting me. He would lean over me, fiercely guarding me in a space of protection that no one dared threaten. This security took my spiritual confidence and bravery to a whole other level, and the channelings then changed to helping exit out dark beings, which first showed themselves to me as wolves. They snarled, snapped, and tried to bite me as they were streamed through my body, only for them be pulled to the ceiling to what looked like a vortex or black hole where they disappeared.

One time there were many bad entities being sucked out through me, for lack of a better description. As one did, it looked at me in complete shock and awe as it passed by. As if he could not believe it was me who was responsible for his removal and I knew how to aid in this process. With this bewildered look on his face, I heard him say, "You?" to which my team replied, "Yes! Her!" My spiritual team beamed in pride, and it was then I realized the work I was doing for the world. Unseen acts I was not able to talk to many about for obvious reasons, but nonetheless, actions and contributions I believe had huge results and were incredibly valuable in their own way. Releases that needed to happen to help cleanse and remove energy from our world to speed up the process and help with mankind's ascension. It was a unique behind-the-scenes role, but I am proud of my contribution and continue to do this healing work to this day. My team lets me know when to change the channelings according to what the world needs at the time, and I wholeheartedly show up for the task.

By now, it's January. I am on the tail end of recovering from my immune flare up. I continued to stay present, trusting the universe had something amazing in store for me as I was completing what felt like the biggest test I had ever endured. I was teaching my spiritual superpower courses, hosting mass meditations, and introducing people to full and new moon rituals as I knew their power surrounding manifesting and releasing.

Then began the next courageous phase of my life, the beginning of something I realize continues to be nothing short of life changing with perfected timing. I had a friend move in, and she was having issues with the school board using harsh chemicals on her children's hands resulting in severe rashes, all without her consent or knowing. This is when I learned of Darren and how he was helping her write up notices to the school board as he was very proficient in law. His true passion and search? Perfecting and claiming people's identity through surrendering their birth certificates. A "coming back to life" through the power of "equity." From the moment I heard those words, my body rang with excitement. I immediately saw all these soul contracts I had with people around this topic. So many people who needed to learn this, something I knew so little about, yet resonated with me to my core. I vibrated just hearing about it and having learned to follow those feelings, I requested to meet him or hoped to arrange a zoom interview.

You can imagine my surprise when he came back with my friend two weeks later after he too had a sense that he had to meet me. That morning, we sat around my kitchen table for the next nine hours as I proceeded to interview and ask him questions about equity, birthright, and what happened around birth certificates. Unbeknownst actions that left us victim to a system where we think we have control and free will but do not. It is the reason the government can take away your house, children, continue to make you pay taxes, and impose their will and rules upon you. COVID-19 clearly rubbed that in our faces; the government can do whatever they want, where we have limited, if any, rights or free will at all. And why is that? Who and what gives them the power? We did! That is the crazy part. We dropped the ball when it came to claiming our identity when we were born. In fact, we did it all backward. Because of this, we have continued to lay victim to a system and form of slavery that we signed up for ironically enough and completely voluntarily!

Darren happily answered all my endless questions, and I was in complete shock and awe about what I was learning. To understand that there is a great secret surrounding my birth certificate with events that happened that resulted in me giving away my power and identity. Although unknowingly, I fell victim to a system of bondage and control where I became the trustee and debtor and left holding the ball.

Keeping in mind legislation from parliament is the same around the world, the Law and Equity Act of British Columbia currently reads under "Equitable relief for defendant Section 5:" "If a defendant claims to be entitled to an equitable estate or right or to relief on an equitable ground against a deed, instrument or contract, or against any right, title or claim asserted by a plaintiff or petitioner in a cause or matter, or alleges an equitable defense to a claim of the plaintiff or petitioner in the cause or matter, the court, whether as a court of law or equity, and every judge of it, must give to every equitable estate, right or ground of relief claimed,"... con't

Brief overview: *Once we perform a few necessary conditions, according to "Securities law" we can bring simple evidence(s) to a Court, for a simple hearing; and whereby, a Judge will approve special instruments of Title that may be registered at: Land Titles, and, by a Court order: Instruct the Registrar-General to record this special Court order. The nature of this special event just changed your life. A welcoming back to it.*

The three of us were inspired to start a company called "Dievergent5" after Darren drafted the paperwork for my friend and me to voluntarily surrender our birth certificates and all our ID to the attorney general. We even affixed a value to it by attaching a one ounce piece of silver, and we received a favorable response back. We are now the first two people in BC to change our names, birth dates, and receive proof of a time dated stamp on a "PPSA Security Agreement" from land titles, showing we now gained "Private Citizenship." We are considered "Protected

To Be Brave

Purchasers" aka "Assets and Friends to the Crown/Queen," and we recently submitted paperwork to the courthouse only to have more success in gaining acceptance into "Chancery Court" (once thought to not exist), where we currently await our court date. I applied for my "white passport," and we have done multiple videos on the subject on our YouTube channel, drawing in people from all around the world. Many have helped us set up our website, translating the documents into different languages, and uploading their legal documents for people to use at no cost and all by donation. We are collaborating with many lightworkers and warriors from around the world to help people redeem their identity and give them the tools in which to do it. A true coming together of like-minded people with a common interest and genuinely based in love. True perfection!

My next brave step happened in the middle of February of 2021, when I was asked by my team to quit my job of almost twenty-three years. I knew why they were asking this of me; it was the last 3D cord I needed to cut, and it was a big one. It had supported me, kept me safe, and offered a very lucrative income. But how could I ask others to trust this new information if I didn't trust it myself? I could play it safe and wait until I saw the prize and knew it worked for sure, or I could jump and trust the universe was going to catch me based on how it felt. The answer was easy, and on March 1st, 2021, I quit. It was not even scary to do, either. I had such a "knowing" inside of me; there was no other way or decision I could have made. There was a reason I had attracted all of this.

Now, here I am not even two weeks later, being asked to write this chapter and share my story with all of you. My heart and soul could not be fuller. The blessings and happiness I continue to experience as I show up for what is being asked of me cannot be put into words, and I look forward to sharing more of these truths with the world because all is not lost. Not even close! In fact, we are just getting started, and we have Covid to thank for that. As a collective, we created the emergence of this energy; it couldn't have happened any other way. Although it has had its heartbreaking moments, we will soon be able to look back and see why this all happened, exactly as it did, and all by design. Nothing happens by accident, and the universe has perfect timing. Until then, I will continue to shine my light through Dievergent5, show up when I am called, and rise to this 5D energy we are becoming "awakened and alive" to understanding.

About Jodi Lynn:

Jodi Lynn - Protected Purchaser

Her current role: Security Entitlement Holder - controlling a financial asset directly

Her company is Dïevergent5, and her title is Beneficial Interest Holder enjoying Life Estate RN# 480-666-025. Her goals and aspirations are to affect the Jubilee globally; releasing debtors under a Mortgage in Equity.

Her greatest most impressive achievements to date: waking up to an illusion that has ensnared the globe, unknown to most. She understood she was at the right place at the right time to receive incredible wisdom and knowledge and maximized these events. She is currently navigating Caesar's realm and through her "surrender" she has indeed rendered unto Caesar.

Her quirky fact? She talks to angels and ET's!

Our info:
Website: divergent5.com
YouTube: Divergent5
Facebook Page: Dievergent5

Chapter Seven

A Voice for the Voiceless

By Sarah Choujounian

I'm originally from Montreal, but I have been living in Toronto for over twenty years now. I haven't had the easiest life and had to overcome many obstacles to get to where I am today. It's been a tough ride, but I have absolutely no regrets and believe all of it was worthwhile as it made me into who I am today.

As a young child, I was a victim of incest which opened the door for many other instances of the same type of abuse. I also had a very difficult time with my parents separating when I was eight. I was a kind, sporty, and anxious kid. I never really fit in because I was a tomboy; nobody knew it then, but this was due to the sexual abuse I had endured. As a teenager, I begged at the subway and sold drugs in order to afford the weed and alcohol to fuel my addictions. There were many more instances of all kinds of abuse during this period. By the time I hit seventeen, I was ready to die.

It was around this time that I met my husband to be, who had appeared to be the savior I was then subconsciously looking for. At the tender age of eighteen, I became pregnant and married this man who was fifteen years older than me and claimed to be a refugee. He was deported shortly after, and we struggled to get his papers for the next eleven years. He became increasingly abusive throughout the years, therefore I had a choice to make: be a victim for the rest of my life or face my problems head on.

The first time I really stood up for myself was when I left my abusive husband and decided to raise my three kids on my own. It was petrifying, as I didn't know if I would be able to make it financially. I also knew my addictions were now once again active, and I was petrified of my ex harming us, as he had threatened to kill me and came close to doing so once before. What if I left and made my kids' life worse instead of giving them the peaceful loving abuse free home I craved for them to have?

I remember the moment when everything became clear. I was staying with him because I thought having a father figure around would mean they would have a better life than I did. One day, as I was crying due to some domestic event that had happened, my eldest, who was ten at the time, held my hand and asked me why I stayed with him. She told me she wasn't happy and often thought of running away. That was the turning point for me; something clicked in my head that day. I remember it becoming very clear that I had to leave no matter what. I was ready to die for my kids to have a "normal" childhood. Within a month of having that conversation, I had taken my girls and left.

My fears of not making it were not in vain. It was very difficult, especially at first. I had to work sixty hours a week to make ends meet. I fell right back into drinking and smoking, and I was dragged into a difficult divorce. I often feared for our safety, and I sometimes thought I wouldn't be able to pull through, but I did. I faced my fear. I was petrified, but I went ahead and did what I had to do to break free from the abuse and give my kids the safe, peaceful life they deserved.

I believe this phase of my life to have been one of the most empowering ones. Facing and overcoming such an immense obstacle made me so much stronger on so many levels. That was one of the biggest lessons of my life. I now always do what's right instead of what is easy. I always listen to my heart and gut feeling instead of my brain. It's crucial for me to always stand in my truth in order for me to be well. My mental and physical health deteriorate as soon as I don't. I strongly believe it's the same for everyone. Standing up for what I believe in has become one of the most, if not the most, important mission in my life.

After surmounting the tremendous stress brought on by my divorce and having somewhat successfully managed three kids on my own, I became extremely empowered. I took leading positions like president of the school council and chief steward of the union at work. Around that same time, I started having many physical ailments: joint and muscle pain, IBS, interstitial cystitis, I felt bugs crawling on my skin, had memory loss, was losing balance, and I was overcome with an extreme fatigue that I still don't have the proper words to explain today. I was literally falling apart. I did so many tests which all came back normal, and my doctor informed me it was all in my head. That was when I decided to take my own health in my own hands.

As I waited to see a neurologist, I did some research and concluded I had fibromyalgia. It was then confirmed by the specialists. I bluntly refused the drugs that were offered to me, as I knew very well they were just band aid treatments I would become tolerant to until no higher dose could be prescribed. I would end up in crippling pain for life.

Instead, I decided to get help from The Gatehouse, a safe place for survivors of sexual abuse. Their programs were so effective that within less than a year, I got completely clean, lost sixty pounds, no longer had most of my fibromyalgia symptoms, and I had learned how to effectively manage the CPTSD that had been running my life. My transformation was so outstanding that I not only became a facilitator at The Gatehouse, but I also founded "Lighting Up Dark Corners" to empower survivors to heal and rise. I was on a mission to share what I had learned in order to help others overcome somatic illnesses and mental health issues by going to the root of their problems instead of being medicated, which infringes the healing process.

When the first lockdown took place in March 2020, I was already known to be the voice of the voiceless. I had been working in long-term care for the greater part of my career. It was always quite obvious to me that the purpose of nursing homes is not to give our elderly the best care possible, but to get a large profit out of them. That's why a huge alarm went off in my head the day the government announced we were shutting down the economy to protect these same vulnerable people.

Things didn't add up, and I could tell right away the lockdowns were much more detrimental to the health of our society than the virus itself. At first, I thought no one would buy it, but then I realized everyone did and that people, like the union, were gaslighting me into feeling as though I was in the wrong. I stayed quiet for a while, fearing losing my job and literally wondering if I was the one who had lost her mind as my mental health declined substantially. When the second lockdowns hit, I could no longer take it. Oppression has always been one of my biggest triggers, and there was no escape from its presence everywhere I looked. It came to a point where I felt like I was going to blow up; I had no choice but to take a stand for what I believed in. I was propelled to stand up and speak my truth, for the first time, at a freedom protest in Toronto on December 31st, 2020. I also founded Nurses Against Lockdowns.

Since then, I was terminated from both my nursing jobs and my license is under investigation. I was also portrayed as a dangerous conspiracy theorist and defamed by the mainstream media, which in return brought in a surge of online abuse and threats. I even had the RCMP knocking at my door asking me about our trip to Washington D.C. where we spoke at a health and freedom summit. This in no way has deteriorated my passion for advocating for medical freedom, and I have absolutely no regrets. If I had the chance to start over, I wouldn't change any of it. The love and support I have received outweighs the negative attention by far.

Presently, I am working on building our grassroots organization called "Canadian Frontline Nurses." This organization has the goals of uniting nurses, educating the public, and bringing ethics back into healthcare. We are very excited about it and envision a future with a bigger focus on preventative care, more natural healing, and the well-being of a person as a whole.

A question people ask me often these days is "How did you discover the courage to speak up?" People think being courageous means the lack of fear, which is absolutely wrong. Courage is the act of doing something even though you are terrified to do it. It's a no brainer for me. I've been here before; I have experience with being uncomfortable and petrified of doing something but doing it anyway because I know it's the right thing to do. When I left my ex-husband, there were many times where I feared for my life. By overcoming that situation, I learned that on the other side of fear and discomfort lives peace, growth, strength, and wisdom.

When people ask me what they can do themselves to stop these tyrannical measures from continuing, I recommend they simply stop complying. This can all end today if we all decide to stop. People need to be aware that these measures are not only harmful, but they are also illegal. The mandates go against our Charter of Rights and Freedoms; therefore all the fines do not stand in court.

Throughout history, when the government took something away from the people, they never willingly gave it back. The people always had to gather and protest in order for them to get anything in return. The globalists are now in the process of implementing The Great Reset and Agenda 2030, a plan that would not be well received by the public if not introduced with a Trojan horse like the coronavirus. We are on the path of losing all our freedoms and liberties, therefore it is imperative that we stop complying. There's a quote taken from one of my speeches that really seems to have caught attention, and it's something I really want people to grasp: "Revolutions are never easy and require sacrifice, but losing our jobs and material things are nothing compared to losing our rights and freedom for the upcoming generations."

The time has come for each and every one of us to stand in our power. You are the hero of your story; you decide what's going to happen to you. Please do not let fear and hate take over our humanity. Spread love and don't ever stay silent in the face of oppression. The world needs for you to be awake and stand up for what is right. It starts with you. Together we will overcome, and we will rise through the ashes of the matrix.

A Voice for the Voiceless

About Sarah Choujounian:

Sarah Choujounian has been a nurse since 2004 and has been working in a nursing home for the greater part of her career. In 2017, she was diagnosed with fibromyalgia which was the catalyst for her life-changing actions. Through natural healing, she was able to get completely clean, lost sixty pounds, and healed herself from most of her fibromyalgia. She has done extensive research on psychology and trauma and initiated an organization called "Lighting Up Dark Corners" to empower survivors. She is known to be the voice of the voiceless, and she intends to keep it that way. She is now the cofounder of Canadian Frontline Nurses, an organization aimed at uniting nurses and keeping their oath to do no harm by speaking up against these draconian measures and restoring medical freedom. She envisions a future where healthcare is based mainly on preventative care, natural treatments, and treating the person as a whole – meaning caring for mind, body, and spirit as one.

www.CanadianFrontlineNurses.com

Chapter Eight

Brave Story

By Sherry Roy

My name is Sherry Roy. I am a Canadian, born and raised on a farm in Ontario, and my parents still live in the homestead where my sisters and I grew up. After graduation from the University of Toronto in 1981, I moved west to Calgary where I worked as a social worker for the Alberta government for five years. Rocky Mountain weekend destinations were my favorite, and so many amazing memories were created there.

In 1986, I was planning to move home to Ontario, as I was missing my family, as well as the Ontario waters and trees. I decided to take a summer detour and move to Vancouver and take in Expo 86. In the fall of 1986, I met my husband Dave and his two children, Jennifer, four years old, and Bryan, three years old. Dave and I will celebrate thirty-four years of marriage on June 20th, 2021.

Today, we have four children: Jennifer, born in 1982, Bryan, born in 1983, Sarah, born in 1988, and Jeremy, born in 1991. We live on an acreage in Armstrong, BC, where we have lived for almost twenty years. So far we have ten grandchildren, and what a blessing they are.

I've always been outspoken, often saying, "I've been blessed with a voice and the courage to use it." It has not always been easy. However, I knew and know it's important to be brave, stand up, and be an example to not only my children, but to the community. Be the example of what's possible. Be the change we need and want to see in the world.

When I met Dave, Jennifer and Bryan were sick often, visiting doctors and on antibiotics a lot. I started to question the healthcare system, even looking at my own experiences as a child, youth, and young adult. It wasn't long before I realized ...

There is a difference between health and wellness and disease sick care management.

As so many do, planning a family had me digging deeper and led me to make informed decisions for our family. This is our immunization story.

Our family opted out of vaccination in favour of health and wellness. Lifestyle matters; food and beverage do matter! Our children only saw medical doctors for broken bones and stitches. They were far healthier than their vaccinated peers, and that is still our experience today.

At sixty-three years of age this June 25th, 2021, I myself haven't seen a medical doctor in thirty years or since the birth of our son. We know how to keep our immune system in balance and what to do when it's not. Today my focus is on slowing and reversing the aging process and it shows. I love that! To be honest, I don't know why we go to and put faith and belief in a system that focuses on disease sick care management, if health and wellness are our goals. There is another way to look at this story; it's in our hands.

Walking this journey as long as I have, I knew immediately in March 2020 this wasn't what it seemed. However, I had no idea the extent of the plandemic, so I engaged with all the truth seekers I was already following, such as *The Highwire* with Del Bigtree. I haven't missed an episode since *The Highwire* started. Vaccine Choice Canada-VCC, Sherry Tenpenny, Christiane Northrup, and Pam Popper are others to name a few. We were digging deep and asking the questions we had already been asking for many years.

Following whistleblower Dr. Shiv Chopra, who was the senior scientist with Health Canada from 1968 to 2004, was a blessing for me while our children were growing up because I, too, felt the bullying of many doctors whenever our children were in need of support for broken bones and stitches. I would often be yelled at for not vaccinating our children, to which I would say, "I have different information than you do. If you would like to review the information that led me to make the informed decision that I have, we can have this discussion. If not, there is nothing to discuss." We stopped going to medical doctors unless it was an emergency. It was the best decision I ever made.

As a family counselor/behaviour specialist, I got to witness the psychotropic drugging of children, youth, and young adults under the guise of mental health and the role our education system plays. This left me feeling like I was doing my job with my hands tied behind my back. Lifestyle and nutrition were not part of my mandate. If I wouldn't medicate my own children, how could I help these families? So, I left my job and went back to school at IIN, Institute for Integrative Nutrition, and became a

Certified Holistic Health Coach, where I teach families how to make lifestyle changes.

A year into COVID-19 and the evidence is more and more clear this has absolutely nothing to do with a virus. This *is* the great reset, and it's far from what it appears to be. The more we learn, the worse it gets. The Globalists want total control!

I've never followed COVID-19 rules. Having an acreage allowed me to invite friends and their children over to play privately because we knew how important it was. So many moms expressed heartache that "my friends won't see us." What a joy it was to watch the children do what children do. I remember how happy it made us to watch them and how we kept it private in the beginning to keep everyone safe, not from COVID-19 but from the criticisms of others who were, and still are, living in fear.

Birthdays, Easter, Thanksgiving, Christmas … I bought myself a "Come Back with a Warrant" rug and hosted a 2020 New Year's Eve party. We had an amazing time with great food, beverage, and singing around the fire.

I attend rallies, convoys, and protests weekly. We gather regularly online and in-person to provide support, encouragement, and education so Canadians can step out of fear and into truth. Most of the people I hang out with today I didn't know a year ago. What a blessing that is!

Another blessing is all the things I'm learning that I didn't know before. At every opportunity, I'm watching and listening to experts who I can trust with the truth, so I can feel confident sharing, being an example, and teaching others. Like not wearing a mask anywhere, ever. Educating the public, including businesses, why I have a

The Brave: Courage During COVID in Canada

human right not to wear a mask and how to exercise those rights with confidence, peace, and love, especially when there is push back. I'm so thankful for Canadian constitutional lawyer Rocco Galati and all he and his constitutional rights centres have done to help us get educated. When you know someone like Rocco has your back, it makes this challenging work easier.

By joining groups like #StandUpForFreedom, #NoMoreLockDowns, #VaccineChoiceCanada, #Action4Canada, #HugOverMasks, #MakeCanadaFreeAgain, #FactsOverFears, #WeAreAllEssential, #PoliceOnGuardForThee, #FAFTA FreedomAirway, and Freedom Travel Alliance, we gain the confidence to step into "calls to action," like getting BC human rights blue flyers in every business in BC.

Our grandchildren inspire me to stand up and be brave. However, the recent passing of my mother on February 24th, 2021 has lit a fire under me. My parents have been married for sixty-three years, and it breaks my heart that I cannot be with my dad and sisters at this time. My dad told me, "Don't come home now, Sherry. We cannot have a funeral; we will celebrate Mom in the summer." I will do what I need to do to exercise my right to travel without a mask or doing any testing or quarantining. It's sad to believe we are actually living this way.

As we uncover the truth, the push back from world leaders gets crazier. What I know is this ends when we the people end it.

If not *you*, who?
If not *now*, when?
Rise up, be brave. This is the right side of history.

About Sherry Roy:

Sherry Roy has looked at things differently than most for a very long time. As a graduate of the University of Toronto, BA 1980, working with children and families in a globalist controlled setting had her frustrated on a regular basis, so she stepped outside the box and into a career in Holistic Health Coaching.

The Institute for Integrative Nutrition in New York was her choice for education because it wasn't government controlled content. Sherry Roy aligned herself with The Juice Plus+ Company as a family consumer since 1993 to help bridge nutritional gaps easily and affordably, and to support others doing the same. Today more than ever, growing our own food is essential, and Sherry Roy, after years of tower garden growing, sees JP+ Tower Gardens as an easy, affordable solution.

This COVID-19 experience, like no other before, has been enlightening for many and provides clarity and focus ... the world is thinking differently. It is now time to step with intention into leading by example and teaching how to better take care of ourselves and our families without government rule – what constitutes true health and wellness, learning to grow our own food, what to do with it, how to make our own daily products, how to make our own medicines. Aligning with those like-minded, Sherry

Roy is a believer there are silver linings on the other side of this. Expose and *dismantle* with choices that are more in line with *freedom*.

Sherry Roy JP+ Tower Garden website: https://sherryroy1.towergarden.ca/

Chapter Nine

The Courage to Rise Up

By Paul Allen

I contemplated whether to publish my story or not for many reasons, and my decision to share my journey this past year ultimately came down to one thing – to inspire others. My hope is that my passage encourages someone to speak out, take action, and positively change the course of their life or the world for the better. I want to show people that anything is possible with hard work, love, community, faith in God, and the universe.

I was not like most kids growing up in East Vancouver and Richmond, BC in the 1980s. I questioned literally everything (just ask my parents). I never felt like part of the herd at school or in society and was arguably the black sheep of my clan. In school, I struggled with the indoctrination that suggests good little minions do not "ask questions," "challenge authority," or reason outside of what was taught to us. I always tested the status quo and often did not comply; not because I wanted to rebel, rather the logic made no sense. By the end of elementary school I was aware of the hypocrisy in the "do what I say, not what I do" narrative, and in junior high I struggled to realize how much of what I was learning was of value in life. It reflected in my grades, conflict with teachers, and authority.

The Brave: Courage During COVID in Canada

Curiosity, conscious thought, and critical thinking have been the fabric of my being since I was four years old. Though not received well in public school, it was, in my humble opinion, the root of my many achievements personally and professionally. I have not and will not ever stop being inquisitive. I also feel that my many spiritual and life experiences over the years were all critically important teachings. I needed to receive them at those very specific intervals in my life in order to guide me in the right direction to be exactly where I need to be at this very moment in time.

My two sons are my guiding light and the number one reason I broke my silence in May of 2020, when I participated in my first freedom march at forty plus years young. This after connecting with a beautiful soul from high school who felt the same way about the lockdowns and happens to be an author of a chapter in this book as well. She is a force of activism to be reckoned with that I am in awe of every day. I call her Wonder Woman. We marched and then I delivered my first activist speech from deep within my core to a few hundred fellow freedom supporters citing the media and governments long track record of lies, deception, and creating fear in its people to control them.

I was terrified at the time that my employer would find out, but I needed to do it for my conscience and my children's future. When my speech was finished, applause and cheers followed and I felt truly alive. I was buzzing and excited more than ever for what was to come, more so than any anxiety about losing my well-paid corporate job. I worked for Napa Auto Parts (UAP Inc.) and was responsible for fourteen corporate stores in BC and the Yukon, along with a team of account managers. This was my dream job that I worked fifteen years to secure, but this was bigger than any "job." It is about our future and what we will not tolerate from government, companies, and global elitists who pretend to care about us when all they care about is money, power, and protecting their own interests.

Once I attended my first rally, I was hooked on the people and community, so I continued to attend every other week when I could. I knew there was a risk of getting on the news and my company not aligning with my freedom fight. I figured as long as what I was doing did not involve the brand and was legal, I would be protected. Well, as the months went by and things got worse with no end to the lockdowns, I got more involved. I connected with many amazing groups such as Hugs Over Masks, No New Normal, and countless other amazing individuals who have put their heart and souls into stopping this tyranny. Without my influence, my oldest son even started speaking at rallies as he, too, was fed up with the nonsense at school and fear in the community by the media.

On December 5th my son and I were scheduled to speak at a mega rally, and this one ignited the media's attention as organizers confirmed Canucks anthem singer Mark Donnelly would perform Canada's song as he, too, was questioning the logic behind these lockdowns. At some point a few days before, despite using pseudonyms, my full name was leaked to the media as a speaker. I woke up that morning to a message from my colleague asking me if I was speaking at an "anti-mask" rally to which I replied, "No. I am speaking at a freedom rally." He called me to persuade me not to speak, as the "optics" would not look good, as he put it. After great consideration and only hours before the event, I chose to speak. I rewrote my speech to be more politically correct and talked about kindness, health, wellness, and the toxic lamestream media. Quite tame compared to what I had prepared, but I knew they were watching. After a week or so, my GM blindsided me with a "touch base" video call that ended up being him and our HR manager to discuss my speech. He even had the freedom rally video to show me that I suspect the same employee forwarded to him "concerned for the safety of my teams," as he put it. They had no grounds for dismissal, so I maintained my position about how I spend my personal time and whom with. My boss told me it had to stop; UAP was not okay with it and I needed to stay out of the media, which I did.

Another roadblock with Napa was they began intensifying the mask push, which I had managed to avoid for months due to medical reasons. I was told that I needed to wear one, and it was mandatory, even with my health concerns. Once I read the policy thoroughly, the words did not say it was "mandatory" so I contested it. I was told yet again that I had no choice but to wear one when in any Napa building, so I went and saw my doctor who agreed I should not wear a mask if I felt my breathing was constricted. My boss stood down and told me I did not have to go into any building until this was over, which I thought was naïve as most of us lions knew this was not going away anytime soon. Things changed moving forward, and I felt the romance was over. I increased sales by 20% in arguably one of the toughest years on record and was regarded as one of the top managers in the company, yet I suddenly felt like the adopted stepchild.

On December 30th, 2020, I was advised we had an internal audit and was asked to do something I did not feel comfortable doing that would affect my team's budget and potentially their year-end bonuses. I was ethically not okay with this and vocalized it heavily. That night, after having to deliver this information to my team, I did something minor in my opinion and personal in relation but silly, and Napa in Atlanta found out about it and used it as a breach of conduct. It was not even something that violated conduct guidelines, but they were done with me because of the rallies and masks (in my opinion) and let me go January 6th, taking a chance I would not sue them.

This cemented my commitment to the cause and fight against companies like Napa who only care about money. They would often preach about people being their biggest assets, which contradicted everything I witnessed from a senior management perspective within the company over eighteen months. As soon as I did not look good for their "brand," as my boss put it, I was disposable. I always knew it was a load of shite but this time it landed at my doorstep. This cancel culture has to stop, and I am now aligning myself with businesses and opportunities where I have no owners, no obligation to tow the company line when I do not morally agree with something, and now have the ability to fight for what is right without fear of intimidation.

Even an hour after I was let go, I felt liberated, free of the chains of corporate ownership, circle jerk emails, and meetings that should have been emails. I felt *free* and literally was having conversations about partnerships and investment opportunities that afternoon. I decided to take some time to smell the roses, spend time with my sons, and spiritually align myself for the next chapter, as I had not had a work sabbatical in nearly thirteen years.

The Brave: Courage During COVID in Canada

Today, I am writing these words on day one of spring break here at the Big White Ski resort an hour outside of Kelowna, BC, Canada with my two amazing boys who are ten and twelve. We could have gone anywhere but we chose Big White, as we have never been but also because the government told me we were not allowed to do so. I drove here from Vancouver in my latest protest of the nonsensical lockdowns and illegal travel restrictions imposed on Canadians.

After booking, I was concerned the resort's website seemed like a government sponsored poster puppet commanding the storyline of heavier than required mask enforcement, as well many outdoor activities such as ice skating, tubing, and night time fires that were suspended in the name of COVID-19. I complained to management via email, accusing the resort of being motivated to suspend these services to save money all in the disguise of public safety, not to mention breaking the law by not allowing mask exemptions.

I did not expect my email to gain the attention of the VP of Big White, Michael J. Ballingall, but it did. He offered to refund my stay if I was not satisfied with what they were doing. I politely declined, electing to gauge the whole experience and have the option of sharing my feedback after which seemed worth the $1,500 investment. We went back and forth in a few emails, and I quickly realized this misinformation was coming right from the top.

I was willing to bend with balaclavas on the mountain to avoid conflict, but I assumed with documentation on exemptions conflict could be avoided through a calm, educational approach when indoors for my kids under twelve. I could not have been more wrong. Within seconds of entering the store with a shield on my face (to avoid a clash), three staff members immediately surrounded us, raised their voices at me and my boys as if we had guns, and demanded my sons put on masks or leave. It could not have been more Nazi like.

When I attempted to reason with their manager and educate her on exemptions, she told me there were no exemptions at Big White; kids over two had to be masked. I struggled to educate her as she and the others had no interest in hearing me, only talking over me. I advised them that kids under twelve are not required to wear a mask and encouraged her to go to the BC Government website to validate what I was saying. She refused and told me company policy trumped any exemption including the Charter of Rights and Freedoms and BC Human Rights Code. I told her you could ask someone to leave, just not for this reason; this was discrimination. The boys then waited outside while I bought the balaclavas.

I came back to the ski store before leaving the resort once we had checked out to drop off the government issued literature (without my boys), this time exercising my own exemption not to wear a mask and recording the session as I had no faith in the training they had received from Michael, a self-proclaimed "COVID-19 Resort Expert" on LinkedIn. At this point, my emails with Michael were not going anywhere, and he, too, maintained they had the authority to override exemptions. I felt if their boss was not going to tell them the truth about the laws they were breaking and that they were participating in child abuse, it was up to me to do so in a respectful manner so it did not happen to another parent.

Again, within seconds of walking into the store six to eight staff surrounded me looking like they were going to tackle me. I calmly asked for the manager, explaining why I was there and what I wanted to communicate with them. They escalated things very quickly (the entire interaction was recorded and shared on social media). I stated to all of them very clearly that what they did to my son was illegal, and I wished to leave the material with them so it did not happen again.

At that very moment, the VP of Big White, Michael J. Ballingall who I had never met before, came in yelling my first name at the top of his lungs from across the building. He came up behind me and assaulted me on camera while trying to grab my phone. He attempted to physically remove me from the store, all for dropping off government issued COVID-19 literature to their staff that they were not communicating to patrons. This reinforced my commitment to standing up for me and my family's rights and educating my fellow humans in a kind, compassionate, and respectful way. It is also sadly the one-year anniversary of the assault on our freedoms with no end in sight, so I feel like I have no choice; I need to turn up the volume. We are a year past "two weeks to flatten the curve," graduating into triple masks and anal swabs all for a flu virus with a 99% recovery rate. Is this sinking in yet?

I do feel so incredibly blessed for the opportunities in the past few months and would not reset back to mid-2019 for all the world's gold. I have such gratitude for all the amazing people I have met over this past year and am truly honored to contribute to this project in the pursuit of waking others up to be brave enough to stand up and protect our freedoms. I feel it is my duty to shine a light on the true impacts of COVID-19 to myself, my family, my career, our children, small businesses, mothers, fathers, nurses, doctors, first responders, and everyone else who has been silenced, threatened, or lost their livelihoods due to this plandemic.

The impacts of the lockdowns are a guesstimate to be twelve to one. That means for every one person (god bless them) who has died of COVID-19, not "with" the virus (as that is very different and not a "true" COVID-19 death) but from it, twelve other lives are heavily impacted by unemployment, financial hardship, substance abuse, depression, domestic violence, suicide, postponed surgeries, and countless other diseases. The saddest casualty of all is, in my opinion, the isolation of seniors now dying from loneliness, aka a broken heart. It does not have to be this way.

These words are for anyone without a voice or who has been intimidated for speaking out against this madness while big corporate giants like Walmart and Amazon continue to operate unaffected and are thriving more than ever, increasing their net worth to record levels. Let that sink in; while an estimated 200,000 businesses close this year in Canada, record profits are being reported from companies like Costco and Loblaw's that sell the same products as stores that are forced to close. It is just wrong. We all need to be brave, be strong, and have the courage to stand up and say *no more* to unlawful lockdowns, government tyranny, and this bought and paid for fake news media narrative.

We need to stop complying and being complicit in these crimes against humanity. Take off the mask, unplug from mainstream media and Hollywood influence, break up with your owners (or anyone who forbids you to speak out), listen to your own mind, and get healthier. Sleep well, eat well, exercise, and be cautious of whom you share your time with and what you allow into your mind, body, and soul. Be brave. Most of all, just be you. Be the best version of yourself you can be, and I will vow to do the same until my time on this planet is complete.

I have always had a strong drive to uncover the truth and communicate it to others, and now is my time to shout it to the world. We are the people; we are all essential, and we will have the courage to rise up and fight until we succeed. Non-negotiable. My Great Uncle Rob Roy and many others fought and died for Canada during WWII for our freedoms, and I will be damned if I give them up that easy. I will fight for myself, my children, humanity as a whole, and I will not give up until we the people regain our freedom of choice, thought, expression, movement, and speech. Thank you.

About Paul Allen:

Brian (Paul Allen) is a sovereign human, father to two amazing boys, friend, truth-seeker, Canadian patriot, resident of planet Earth, and advocate for those who are not able to stand up for what we know is wrong for the community, the earth, and humanity. He is just getting started. Brian's journey started in Hamilton, Ontario, and then moved to Vancouver, BC. Brian spent his first five years in East Vancouver and grew up in Richmond from age five until he left to see the world at age twenty. Well, some of it anyway, including visiting Scotland to soak up his Scottish ancestry.

After graduating from Langara College with a diploma in Marketing and Sales, he worked with startup Sleep Country, then moved to Calgary to work for WestJet Airlines, Brinks Ltd., Kingsdown, and in 2015 joined Acklands-Grainger. Brian attended Royal Roads University in Victoria, British Columbia, earning a Bachelor of Commerce in Entrepreneurial Management in 2016 before he was recruited to join UAP Inc. in 2019 as a regional sales manager for BC and the Yukon. Brian was responsible for the success of fourteen stores and a team of account managers.

Brian left corporate life at the end of 2020 to pursue his passion of bringing people joy and smiles through entrepreneurship and to commit more time to his boys, activism, the quest for free speech, freedom of choice for body, self, family, and religion in this beautiful country of Canada. Brian continues to advocate for rights and freedoms as the communications coordinator for We Are All Essential, and newly appointed public relations manager for the Freedom Rallies. Brian plans to continue the fight in whatever capacity he can until the rights and freedoms are returned to Canadians and the world. Won't stop, can't stop.

Chapter Ten

The People's Truth

By Amanda Forbes

This isn't a chapter about a leader, or someone more brave or special than anyone else. This is just my story, the story of a wife and mother who has had enough of the constant division and lies being spoon-fed to the Canadian population by a broken system and increasingly corrupt government. A fight to protect and hold onto the things I hold dear and to take back what has been lost for the sake of my children, and everyone's children, while also fighting to keep what remains of Canada and our freedoms for *all*.

My journey started well before 2020. It was a vaccine injury that almost took our youngest child from us, a reaction that completely blindsided our family - not once, but twice. Two separate reactions after two different well-baby visits. The second occurrence was what jolted us awake to what was occurring in the allopathic health care system. The mantra of "Safe and Effective" we once used to recite to the other "tinfoil hat wearers" was now 100% proven to be just a pharmaceutical tag line for their clever marketing agenda. That magical medical mantra almost cost us our child's future. Her forever. Just like that, we became ex-vaxxers. In an instant my family's belief system was turned upside down, an immediate jolt from "The Matrix," if you will.

The Brave: Courage During COVID in Canada

Years ago I found myself in a fight for truth, health freedom, and advocacy that I never in a thousand years would have believed I would be a part of, let alone help lead.

During my journey, I found myself being drawn to new soul tribes, which led me to a wonderful group of fighters in America known as The Vaxxed Team. It was there my advocacy exposure really picked up. I founded Vaxxed Canada, and with the help of some of the most wonderful people across our great country, we premiered the highly controversial film called *Vaxxed 2: The People's Truth*, in order to bring awareness to people across Canada about the risks and dangers of vaccines. During this time, we faced some very complicated backlash of government division tactics, as well as threats to our screening vendors of permanent closure from public health officials should they follow through with showing the film.

In hindsight, this film was a *massive* "red pill" for many people who had the pleasure of seeing it. Considering we wrapped up our screenings in March of 2020, the push against us then now made perfect sense. Those who saw the film were those who saw through the COVID-19 agenda very quickly.

Today, I am still highly involved with the Vaxxed Team and continue to work very closely with Polly and Toby Tommey, Brian Burrowes, and the rest of the Vaxxed family.

In August of 2020, I was asked to start the process of bringing Children's Health Defense to Canada. An amazing organization headed up by RFK Jr., Mary Holland, and other beautiful warriors who stand to protect the health of all people and end the childhood epidemics to eliminate harmful exposures and hold those responsible accountable. To establish safeguards so none of this ever happens again to us or our children. This cause is so incredibly close to my heart.

Most recently, however, you will find me teamed up with Tania the Herbalist, Danielle Pistilli, and Alicia Johnson in order to bring The Freedom Organization to Canada. A group dedicated to empowering others, educating all, and helping every single Canadian citizen find ways to take action and have their voices heard.

The Freedom Organization's Freedom For Truth Conference was derived as a way to bring everyone opposed to Covid measures together to make their numbers count without the risk of losing their livelihoods or friends. It's a way to take action for your country without a stipulation of fear associated with participation. It's a sad state of affairs when that has to be a concern for *any* Canadian!

Prior to the "pandemic," I was a person who was of the mind set to "live and let live." Your way of life doesn't affect me personally, and mine shouldn't be a concern for you, either. However, I have always had the tendency to stand up for others before I stand up for myself. Perhaps that comes from the contentment I have found within, because I have made peace with my decisions and where I am in my journey long ago. Contentment surrounds me the majority of the time.

I feel I was lucky enough to be prepared for the "pandemic" from the get go. Being involved in the Health Freedom Fight, we already *knew* to be prepared for an "outbreak" of some sort. Most advocates knew about Agenda 2020/30 and the Sustainable Development Goals of the NWO for years. Which now many others who are joining in 2020 see as well. It has become almost comical to see how fast people realized it once COVID-19 hit. Before 2020, discussing anything in this regard was crazy and would immediately qualify one as a "tinfoil hat wearing quack" – and yet here we are *living it* – in full colour.

The great thing about all of this, in my opinion, is I believe they truly underestimated humanity on a grand scale. They thought everyone would go down without a fight against the "invisible enemy," but they were wrong. What was to be The Great Reset very quickly became The Great Awakening, and it continues to be an incredible thing to witness. All of us have a front row seat to watch history be made. Here and *now*.

Another silver lining out of this whole thing for me was the fact that it simplified home life and brought the family unit together tighter than ever. I loved that my family slowed down and spent much more needed quality time together, and we learned to re-appreciate that time. We all learned to listen to the heart and soul again, for which I am very grateful.

In the beginning, our family did what every other family did. We played our part to stay home and save lives for the infamous "two weeks to flatten the curve." We did this for probably two to three months, to appease outside family members, but I was, and continue to be, very fortunate to have the incredible benefit of being connected to some of the best and morally ethical doctors, scientists, and lawyers in the world. I knew if they were questioning things, everyone else should be as well.

Never before in human history have we locked down like this. Not even for diseases with a higher death count or those that continue to have higher death counts than COVID-19 every year.

Case and point: tuberculosis. People need to ask themselves *why*? Why isn't the fear factor the same for TB? The answer is simple ... there is *no* vaccine in the pipeline for TB yet. Also, the media isn't blasting a fear campaign at the request of the government 24/7. Not on the tel-LIE-vision, not on the radio, not posted in every bus stop and window ad, or every daily newspaper. They aren't attaching the national anthem to fight against TB, so you don't feel it is your patriotic duty to "protect others" from it. This is government manipulation, and way too many Canadians are succumbing to it.

People have forgotten kindness and humanity because they allowed fear to absorb them from head to toe. The government called for people to start calling snitch lines on neighbours and encouraged divisive actions by allowing citizens to become violent with others for opposing completely *legal* views. All the while knowing *none* of these emergency orders could *ever* supersede the Canadian Charter of Rights and Freedoms. They knowingly allowed a society of division to occur.

Do you find it a coincidence that there is *always* a marketing *fear* campaign to a "deadly disease" when there is a vaccine in the pipeline or sales numbers are needed? Just ask yourself where the flu and measles went last year. They were "deadly" the year before. Everyone *needed* that vaccine before COVID-19. Not so much now. Not a peep about it since the start of school season 2019 and very minimal discussion in 2020. *Your fear of a given disease is always proportionate to the quantity of pharma and government advertising in any given year.*

At the beginning of COVID-19, I waited with a heavy heart to see our people in Canada start dropping in the streets like they did in China. To my surprise, that never happened. I waited to hear of people dying of COVID-19 in their homes, but that didn't happen either. No one died of COVID-19 unless they were in the hospital or in a LTC facility. Why was that if it was so deadly? Lastly was when the MSM started recycling video clips from America and calling it Toronto. The lack of transparency, truth, and evidence from our government "leaders" this year has been anything but moral, ethical, or trustworthy.

We are all living in what they would have the public believe is one of two categories. Either a country infested by an ever-mutating pandemic that the science clearly does not support, or a "conspiracy life" where government officials continue to gaslight, doxx, or "Wakefield" leading doctors and scientists at every turn.

Those are tactics of a guilty party, criminals in every aspect of the word. Unfortunately, the MSM is a willing and paid off participant in the disinformation campaign that is COVID-19. The constant shifting of the goal posts should be enough for many to wake up, but if it isn't, then maybe it is the involvement of eugenicists Bill and Melinda Gates' in our country's affairs and their direct funding of some of our decision making "top doctors," hospitals, and mayors. Or maybe it is just our PM's romantic relationship with China that sends those sirens off immediately. I have no doubt that everyone will see in their own time, and when the time is right. Of that I am positive. The truth always finds the light, and the light *always* wins!

Nothing I have ever done I ever considered a sacrifice. Everything I do, I do for the sake of my children's freedom and future, as well as for all Canadians that hold the same values. Even those who still don't have the ability to fully *see* the big picture. There will *never* be anything I wouldn't sacrifice for them. The love I have for my children and husband is second to none other than God, and I would risk my entire life to ensure their futures were one of freedom, love, prosperity, and happiness. In turn, I would hope it would teach them to fight like hell to do the right thing for *all* of humanity and to be as selfless and accepting of every person, regardless of their beliefs, language, or ethnicity. Teach them that differing opinions don't automatically make you enemies, but offer new perspectives to life and that name calling doesn't fix anything. Open and honest dialogue will get that job done, but unfortunately the ability is a dying skill in this day and age.

Good people *will* disobey bad laws, and you can see that very clearly throughout history as we cycle through a new type of holocaust. Again, my mindset has always been to live and let live. My life experiences have caused me to take the actions I do as a woman, wife, and mother, just like any other sane person on this planet would. My heart has always had an affiliation to do what is right, what is just, and to always take each step with love in my heart for *all*.

The time has come to overhaul our governments for the betterment of all and remove corruption and tyranny. To create a government that is *for* the people, *by* the people. *All people!* Indigenous, black, brown, white, English and French as *one*. As well to ensure this overreach, deception, and division *never* happens again. To step up and become the kind of Canadians we are *all* proud to be.

A Charter of rights and freedoms remains, but a newly formed Charter, with ironclad protections of freedoms for all citizens, is needed. Sovereign citizens. A government that actually answers to the people and provides results. A Canadian's first philosophy, while remaining true to our Canadian heritage of always being a friend to those in need, after our people are cared for first.

I am no different than anyone else. My life just took a massive detour years ago that forced me to wake up and see the bigger picture sooner than most. I don't live in fear, and I never have. I trust the plan God has laid out for my life, so I live life to the fullest. I have turned off the tel-lie-vision and radios and removed the intentional 24/7 bombardment of "programming" being thrown at everyone and taken responsibility for myself and my family's health.

I turned within for answers and found them! I found my way back to self and stopped looking for approval from the external world. I accepted all that I am and continue to be. The good and the bad. The perfect and the imperfect. Flaws and all, and I decided to help others do the same. With that action, I found a strength even I didn't know I possessed. It gave me enough courage to give a voice to all of the concerns I had, and I allow others a platform to do so as well. I look for ways to bring people the information they need to hear – the other side, the unpopular and uncomfortable truth – and from there they can then decide what is right for themselves.

If it resonates, wonderful. If not, that's wonderful too. But the truth is always felt within. It sets off an emotional reaction within you, whether it be anger, fear, grief, gratefulness, sadness, happiness, being thankful, or what have you. That reaction promotes self-growth in one way or another.

I have never been a rule follower when there was a choice between doing the right thing or doing what I was told, but I will always choose to do the right thing. Everyone's journey is different, and people get to certain places and mindsets in their own time. However, everyone's perspective is important. It's how we grow and evolve as a collective. When you censor one side or another, the disservice is a harmful dictatorial one. Some of us live on the frontline as warriors, others work behind the scenes, some support, and some do it all. Regardless, every one person and their voice is *so* incredibly important in this fight for freedom.

My advice would be to find what works for *you* and have your voice heard through the magic you create. *Empower* your beliefs and make the change you want to see in the world, then *live* it!

Courage absolutely does not mean a lack of fear or even knowing what the process will look like. It just means trusting yourself, your heart, and your intentions and starting. Change is always uncomfortable, risk is always uncomfortable, but the rewards are endless and ongoing. It offers a ripple effect, and if you are lucky, you get to see glimpses of those ripples in time in everything around you.

Go within and learn to listen to your gut, your mind, body, heart, and soul. Eliminate the poisons in your life and environment, physically and mentally. If it doesn't feel good or sit well, get rid of it. Keep only that which serves you and moves you forward in your journey for the better. Practice gratitude and appreciate everything you *do* have. Be conscious of removing any aspect of a "victim complex" you may have and ask yourself what lesson came from this? What did I learn? Instead of placing blame on others, own it and move on. But most of all remember to be humble and always go about every interaction from the heart and with love.

The one thing I would want my children and family to know is that I fought like hell for them, fought for their free futures, and fought for what is right. I fought so they wouldn't have to!

"Let it not be said I was silent when they needed me."

About Amanda Forbes:

Amanda is a retired stay-at-home wife and mom who left the workforce to care for her youngest child many years ago. Today she is a newly homeschooling health freedom advocate who fights passionately for everyone's freedoms.

Amanda founded Vaxxed Canada in 2019 and started The Children's Health Defence Canada in 2021. She is also the co-founder of The Freedom Organization and co-host of The Freedom For Truth Conference, as well as the host of *The People's Truth Canada*.

Amanda works toward the prospect of a transparent and morally ethical government body within a Canada that is unified, removing the service to self-leaders in this country and to embrace a unified collective of good citizen leaders who are not driven by bottom line lobbyists or organizations, but by doing good for all Canadians. Making actual change through unification and knowing the Canadian freedoms as written in The Canadian Charter of Rights and Freedoms is a right of every citizen living off this land. Amanda would like to see new political parties with an emphasis on the people's freedoms.

The Freedom Organization www.freedomorg.ca

Chapter Eleven

Brave AF

By Katy Sinha

I began to learn over twenty-five years ago through a series of unravelling personal memories that fear is a useful feeling that is intended to motivate an action. Either you take flight or you stay and fight.

I was born in Ottawa, Canada and experienced childhood in the early '80s. I grew up feeling blessed that I somehow was lucky enough to be born Canadian and into a decent middle class family. Other than the bumps and bruises that are collected as a result of typical family drama growing up, I received a university education, met my husband, and started our family business together under very "normal" peaceful times. In fact, until 2020, I had a blissfully ignorant and uninquiring sense of luck that I was born in the '70s and our way of life was marked by freedom. After all, we'd been singing our national anthem since kindergarten, "True north strong and free," and I believed every word of it.

A series of early life events caused me to live in a state of fear that neither motivated me to fight or to take flight. I lived in a state of subdued insignificance. It was a state of being that was subtle, easily medicated by distractions, and supported by others who reflected the same dim light. This isn't to say I was apathetic or lazy. I was a competitive athlete in many sports, I loved to ski and canoe with my father, and I had developed a taste for adventure travel. Toward the end of university, I had worked toward the opportunity to lead trips down the Nahanni River in the NWT, Canada. Spending a few consecutive summers being fully absorbed by the magnificence and vastness of this sacred land, while meeting and listening to people from every corner of this earth, had the effect of cracking open my spiritual paralysis that I had been posturing.

I met my husband a few years later, and paradoxically, the closer the relationship I developed with him, the harder it became to respond to life with the fear that had so consistently maintained my inner paralysis. God bless my husband. To this day he is the perfect mirror for me to see my reflection and the quality of its light.

In my twenties, I remember going through a huge emotional unraveling process, sorting out what behaviours I knew no longer served me and what baggage was not mine to carry any further. At this time, I began to hear a voice pierce through my incessant "not good enough" chatter that said to me "*I am on this earth to heal the broken mother - daughter cycles that stretch back many generations.*" Much of my personal growth in my twenties was in the effort to mend the problems from my childhood with respect to my mother.

Then, I was blessed with my first child, a daughter. My world took on a new meaning from that day forward. I knew she was part of the divinity of the universe and a piece of my healing. My beautiful family grew with a second daughter and, within five years, a third daughter! That voice was lighting my spiritual path to raise my daughters with love, presence and in truth, no matter how cult that may be. My path was to become the mother for them that I wished I had known as a child.

With young daughters watching my every move from birth, the highest of my priorities became the art of forgiveness in tandem with focusing on what I wanted to grow in my life. I set out to develop a healthy respect for my body and to weed out the mindset that wished to trap me in a place of diminished self-worth. I had spent a great deal of time nourishing my family with home-prepared meals, teaching my husband and daughters how to cook, what foods to choose for nutrition, and encouraging lifestyle habits to strengthen our bodies naturally. As my daughters grew, I naturally looked for opportunities to introduce them to activities and sports. Like so many families, we were going at full tilt, running our business, raising children, overseeing homework, chauffeuring, and occasionally squeezing in time for our personal hobbies. I am certain I've earned an MDA by now - a Master's in Domestic Administration. My family calls me the "Talent Manager." I chuckle.

Typically, as we were gearing up for my daughter's competitive dance competition, Season Nine, Episode One, March 15th, 2020 came to pass and everything worldwide abruptly stopped. I wrote a passage in my journal after a few weeks of total isolation:

"I am grappling with our collective conscience as I write this. The pressing issue in our souls today is how fearful we are in this Void. We tend to avoid. We have been taught to avoid. Can we see what is contained within this word? A Void. We have been brought face to face with this Void at the same time the world over. It exists within us. Do we avoid within? What are we filling the Void with now? We

collectively slow down, and our essential needs are revealed to us. Good health. Shelter. Fresh food. Love. Clean water. Fresh air. Movement. Connection. Community ... to name a few. What has been let go? What can we let go of that did not serve our essential needs? I recognize that being busy is an impressive shield that can avoid self-reflection, nurture, resilience, play. Will we resume the pace and our consumptive patterns prior to COVID-19 shutdown? Will we rush out to buy more to fill the Void again? Perhaps part of our human conscience is saying "I am sick. I cannot keep up to the demand." We have collectively brought about our own Corrector. A collective lesson to reset ourselves. Notice what is in the Void. We can heal ourselves, our families, our communities, and our planet if we sit in this Void quietly and feel the interconnectedness of all life on this planet. I will continue to reflect and share what I hear from within. Be well." (April 1, 2020)

I decided to run.

I instinctively knew I would need to build a plan for my nervous energy that some people label as fear. Only, I had learned to catalyze fear and allow it to spark an action. I set a BHAG - a Big Hairy Audacious Goal – a fifty kilometers trail run by mid-August 2020. I gathered a small and motivated group of like-minded athletic friends, and we set out week by week training for this BHAG.

The first step was to take the anxious energy and get it moving physically. Keep the energy flowing during this period of stagnant waiting, social media fuelled, watching the prime minister deliver empty Rideau Cottage updates from his front door.

The second step was to tune in. By early April, I got that gut feeling inside that sensed there was something afoot. There seemed to be missing pieces in what was being reported. Death counts, terrifying images, all these horrible mass deaths happening in "hot spots." Again, how lucky we felt to be spared from this horror living in wide open Canada with its sparse population, fresh air, clean rivers, and easy access to nature. I was soaking up social media like a sponge to try and put together what was happening in other parts of the world, and I came across the excellent presentation of two intelligent doctors in Bakersfield, CA during a live press conference they held. These doctors had collected their own data over the previous six weeks directly from their patients and were reporting on that, along with an excellent presentation on the role and function of the immune system. From my estimation and knowledge of the body and immune system health, these doctors were bang on.

All the while, the Canadian "crime" minister was preaching "stay home, stay indoors, stay safe." This was counter-intuitive and contrary advice to everything I knew, spiritually, physically, mentally, and emotionally.

A few days later, to my shock and outright disgust, the doctors from Bakersfield, CA were blocked, censored, and banned from all social media platforms. And so it began, my awakening in April 2020 to the world of illusion and of false idols, of force-fed mainstream media narratives cooked up by shapeshifting oligarchs who own Big Tech, Big Science, and Big Pharma. I had pierced through the veil.

I've since spent month over month awakening to some very dark realizations about this world and how broken, disconnected, and enslaved the people are within this veil. Many tears I have cried for the loss of the country in which I believed was free. Many days I've spent in disgust and anger at the division and loss of humanity reflected in the world today. Admittedly, I've taken every rabbit hole deep dive I've discovered since. My family now calls me "Alice." I have made a conscious effort to look directly at the darkness and to allow it to move me.

I have been unknowingly preparing for this awakening. I look back on all I have learned of who I am. The universe in its intelligent design will always support our growth. I now am bringing into consciousness the full extent of my personal responsibility to hand my daughters a world, a country, and a life worth living in freedom, sovereignty, and dignity. I need only to look into their eyes and feel an overwhelming wave of inspiration to build the courage I need each day.

Today I manage my interactions with others starting with my foundation. I tune in. I ask. How am I doing today on the inside? Am I thinking and interacting with integrity today? Are my actions in alignment with my beliefs? I have learned that although I can tell my daughters how to behave and what to think, they will remember what they saw and they will embody the example I live each day. For instance, having paid attention since April 2020 to the Covid playbook, the actors, and script writers, I knew to prepare for the battleground I would enter simply by refusing to wear a mask while shopping at my local grocery store. I have educated myself on the constitutional laws upon which this country is predicated. I printed out and carried in my purse the municipal by-law of Ottawa and the provincial order in Quebec and familiarized myself in detail with the specifics of the exemptions section.

The Brave: Courage During COVID in Canada

I performed a small ritual prior to entering the grocery store unmasked. I visualized myself with a finely raised vibration, and then I zipped up a gentle area of space around me to help me stay in this space while interacting with the public and store employees. Upon entry, I would be told I had to wear a mask, to which I would compassionately respond that I cannot wear a mask. My response would be met with resistance, so I offered the employee the written section that shows exemptions are permitted. I spoke and showed store managers the written by-law. I followed up with every store's head of customer service to describe the lack of training on the correct application of the by-laws in place, specifically where exemptions are permitted with no need to carry proof. I pressed these service departments to acknowledge my email in a written response. I printed their responses and carried them in my purse. I had to show the grocery store their own head office customer service response to me.

Even with all that groundwork laid, a customer called the police on me while shopping. I again stood my ground. When the Gatineau police officers asked me to show them proof of an exemption, I reminded them that they are offside by asking me to show them any private health information. I did respond by showing them the printed Quebec Order and told them I do not carry anything related to my medical health information as it is a private matter (knowing my constitutional rights). The police officers then told me it didn't matter what the Quebec rules indicated, if the store policy was to remove me, they would be forced to remove me. Having done my homework, I pulled out of my purse the store's corporate customer service statement about honouring exemptions with no need to show proof. The police officers again were not satisfied with this information, so they called the manager over to verify if the information I had produced was legitimate. The store manager (who knew me well by now) regretfully agreed that it is the company's position an exemption would be honoured.

Please make no mistake. My preparation and education for these confrontational conversations made them none the less frightening, for I was nervous like I was giving a speech and shook with adrenaline the minute I was out of the store and all the way home till I cried it out on my husband's shoulder. I felt the fear but the preparation and education allowed me to stand my ground anyway.

That was the experience I needed to evaluate, where instead I would like to buy food for our family. I now regularly source farm to table fruit and vegetable delivery, eggs from a friend, and superb quality locally sourced meats and fish from a kind and reliable fella who brings vacuum sealed, frozen, portioned boxed delivery to my door.

With my family, I ask: Am I caring for my immediate family? What are the impacts of my decisions on my daughters? Are there immediate or short-term risks where I must advocate for their right to body autonomy? Are there long-term risks and if so, how can I promote conversation with them to understand the unveiled nature of the influences and forces at work while they participate in society?

And my dear parents ... have we invited them into our lives to enjoy connection and care? This spring our family will enjoy regular bike riding adventures with Dad, and with Mum in her garden helping her to prepare, plant, care for, and harvest her garden along with outdoor farmers markets building relationships with the local farmers in our area.

In my community, am I standing up and learning how to use my voice? Courage is a muscle that needs exercise. It is an abundantly available power residing within every living soul. Am I using my courage to co-create the future I wish for my daughters and generations to come?

I have come to appreciate the importance of presence today and attention to the lessons of our shared past. Those lessons which were previously learned and since forgotten, by way of distraction, addiction, isolation, fear, paralysis, illness, and disease will be learned again but not without human suffering.

- *"From the moment we are conceived, we have the unalienable right to life in its fullest expression.*
- *Each soul is on a journey of a thousand miles. We know not where the path ends, only the next right step.*
- *Freedom is never given; it is earned over and over with presence and attention.*
- *To overcome darkness we shine our light.*
- *I will never again be worried about what others think, for I now know the bounty of the universe."*

About Katy Sinha:

Born in 1976 and raised in Ottawa, Canada, Katy Sinha completed her double bachelor degrees with honours in Outdoor Recreation and a Bachelor of Arts at Lakehead University in Thunder Bay, Ontario. Her summers were spent leading wilderness river trips on the Nahanni River-and-across northwestern Canada where remote solitude lay the foundation for her spiritual awakening. She then moved in 2000 to her motherland, New Zealand, for two years to begin a deep and ongoing process of growing, learning, and healing.

As fate would have it, on a visit back home to Canada, she met her husband and settled down in Aylmer, QC where they now raise their three daughters. In 2004, they built their Ottawa-based business, Dharma Developments, that today offers specialized land development and construction management services for clients looking to learn and build their own homes. In her spare time she loves to train for difficult challenges like Spartan Beast Trifectas, beginner ultra-running, and is always entertaining the next Big Hairy Audacious Goal.

Chapter Twelve

For Many Are Called

By Danielle Elise Pistilli

"For many are called, but few are chosen" says the Bible, in Matthew 24:14. But what does this mean exactly? I wouldn't necessarily consider myself to be a religious person, but I am deeply spiritual. I definitely feel like the big book has many lessons to teach us. I have to say I have been very blessed when it comes to the doors that have opened up for me through my life, whether it was with a job opportunity, or a promotion, or an opportunity within the company I worked for. Never in a million years did I expect to be called to step into the level of advocacy I see myself partaking in since the COVID-19 shit storm rained down on us all.

On this day, I am sitting down to put fingers to the keyboard, my husband sent me a meme that he felt best described me. It said, "When your family and friends ask you if you *really* have to speak out on the corruption in the world," and you respond with, "Every day. All day. Anywhere. Anytime." Yes, this just about sums me up these days. It is honestly beyond my scope of understanding why people don't want to learn more or why they willfully choose cognitive dissonance over becoming empowered with knowledge. Sadly, this seems to be our current state of affairs. But like many of the leaders across this country, I am lovingly doing my best to stop this runaway train from heading off the cliff anyway I can, despite the criticism, defamatory comments, and the heart-breaking deterioration of lifelong friendships and important family connections.

I would say I have been somewhat of a peacekeeper among my family and friends my whole life. As a manager, within the companies I have worked for, I have always advocated for compromise and collaboration between the staff and the owners of the business, in hopes of inspiring both sides to see another perspective. Surprisingly, I have learned the desire for growth is more for some than others. Personally, as hard as it is to hear someone critique me, I always do my best to take in as much as I can and make a conscious effort to make adjustments where needed.

For twelve years I have been working in a job I manifested for myself, with God's help of course. Somehow, unknowingly, I have always felt that nothing in life happens *to* me ... it happens *because* of me. I now teach about all things holistic, including auras and chakras and the many benefits of colour therapy, aromatherapy, crystals, alchemy, nutrition, prayer, meditation, as well as how comprehending the mind-body connection can help you make subtle changes in your life that can ultimately lead to drastic improvements. When it comes to understanding the colour world, one of the most beneficial aspects has to do with knowing the personality traits of the chakras. This knowledge has helped me to appreciate how people think through their energy strengths and weaknesses. When you comprehend yourself fully, you are better able to tap into certain parts of your personality and work different "energy muscles" to help you achieve the success you desire in life. Put simply, I am a type A personality (high yellow and blue in the colour world). Call me a geek, but I love when there is a place for everything and everything is in its place. One of the hurdles I face is perfectionism. Yes, I am also a Virgo, for those of you who follow astrology. So, when it comes to advocacy and leadership, it has been a huge challenge for me to not care about what others may think when stepping out to this very public arena.

Personally, I have always been a private person. Although I may come across as a "yellow extrovert," my blue energy is more quiet, perceptive, and introverted. Stepping on stage or even doing a live video for social media leaves a lot of room for what, I feel, may be errors and criticism. The anxiety and butterflies around being in the public, even when teaching a small course at work, has almost been debilitating at times. I've spent hours procrastinating and perfecting videos only to talk myself out of launching them for fear of public ridicule. However, each day I am getting stronger and stronger to do what I am doing, and I have some amazing friends to thank for pushing me to step up in ways I never would have before.

For the past five years, I would say I have been a massive learning junkie. There is not a day that goes by where I'm not reading or listening to a documentary, an audio book, or a podcast from someone spiritually inspirational, health related, or some sort of relationship, financial, or success expert. And then there's the one that woke me up! It was a nine-part docu-series called *The Truth About Cancer*. I'll never forget learning what I did from Dr. Robert Scott Bell only ten minutes into the first episode. I was riveted when he explained how the medical industry became so messed up because the Rockefeller and Carnegie Foundations were interested in establishing a medical monopoly by getting a hold of the education system and eliminating all alternative wellness competition. This was the beginning of the rabbit hole for me. I learned there were hundreds of roads to wellness that existed outside of the medical industry and most pharmaceuticals were a cash grab for keeping the public just sick enough so they would forever rely on this industry. Truly, we should be calling this industry "sick care" and not "health care," and I use the word "care" loosely. It's clear that those who drive this ship do not actually "care" for us at all.

One thing I should probably clarify here is that I do believe there are a lot of well-meaning doctors, nurses, and scientists who go into this industry with the full intention of helping people. Sadly, the problem lies with the root of the system, which is a hard concept for medical experts to swallow. To some, this may feel like a personal attack when they have spent their whole lives in this profession. But, if you are a medical expert and you look deep, don't you think it's odd you only get a few hours of classes regarding food and nutrition in *all* your years of training? When 90% of our health care problems are because of the crap we put in our cake holes? Sorry, not sorry to be so brash, but it just doesn't make sense. If someone has cancer, so many oncologists will tell patients it's okay to drink and eat whatever they like when it is a well-known fact that sugar feeds cancer. And why is it that chemo, radiation, and surgery are the only arsenals in an oncologist's toolbox, and if they are to advise an alternative or natural approach, they could lose their licence? These were the questions that were being answered for me in this series, and I highly recommend watching it if you haven't already. It's a definite game changer when it comes to understanding the history of medicine, and it explains a lot about why society is sicker than ever and how it is possible to eliminate the state of dis-ease naturally.

After 2016, my learning curve exploded regarding the cover-ups and lies in the vaccine industry. As a young mother I vaccinated my kids, blindly trusting those in positions of authority to know what was best for them. If anyone reading this isn't sure about whether or not to vaccinate your children, I pray you take the time to investigate the science before you make a decision you may deeply regret. At the very least Google "vaccine injuries" or "vaccine side effects testimonials." You are bound to see parent after parent dealing with their worst nightmare, showing how their child was "normal" one minute and then not the next, following their scheduled vaccination. I wish to God someone had presented me with informed consent regarding my children's vaccines. It wasn't until years later that I learned the life-threatening Kawasaki disease my daughter developed, at two and a half years of age, is a well-known side effect of a couple of different shots.

To this day it makes me sick and brings me to tears to remember holding my daughter down and telling her to "suck it up" and "stop being a drama queen" during her grade nine shots. This may very well go down as my most shameful mother moment. I remember questioning the nurse if the Gardasil vaccine was really necessary or beneficial, and I was told the benefits would way outweigh the downfalls as it would supposedly prevent cervical cancer. There was no mention of side effects or reading the insert, just "trust her." Having just lost my mother-in-law a few years before to uterine cancer, it didn't take much to convince me this needed to be done. So, I pushed my motherly instincts aside and held Madi down while she squirmed and cried due to her massive fear of needles (from the trauma of being held down in the hospital for blood work when testing for Kawasaki). Something else I regretfully didn't pay attention to at the time. Knowing what I know now, about the short and long-term side effects of this absolutely horrific vaccine, I can only pray that I haven't ... Honestly, I can't even write down what I fear because I am a big believer in the power of words. I am just going to stop and continue to pray for her continued health. I am happy to say I woke up before my son's grade nine vaccines and was elated when my son later told me that one of the hockey dads, who I shared *The Truth About Vaccines* series with, had also opted out of having his son vaccinated. It was only one person, but the joy I felt knowing I had awoken at least one person was absolutely soul-lifting. Little did I know, this would only be the beginning.

The few years leading up to 2020 have, undoubtedly, trained me and my family for what we were unknowingly about to step into. As a mom, I taught my kids to be open-minded to the world of alternative thinking and was proud when my kids could see when something wasn't right. They are not afraid to speak up and question the authority of those who have treated them unfairly or when teachers have failed to do their jobs effectively. I guess you could say I have been teaching them to "work their blue energy," or in other words, to be polite but don't be afraid to stand up for yourself. Let's face it; there's many people in authoritative positions who don't deserve the respect they demand. I think it's important to let our kids know that just because a person is in a position of authority, that doesn't always make them right, nor do you always need to conform to what the masses think.

I'd say there are a lot of out-of-line, under-educated mask police in society, but I'm thrilled Madi and Keaton know how to stand up to any adult violating their rights. I am pretty sure my son is one of the first kids in high school who is not wearing a mask and didn't provide an exemption letter. What we did provide was a six-page human rights letter stating he has an exemption, and the school has no right to request proof of it despite their insistence and their shockingly discriminatory comments. We could have just provided the letter, but then no one would have learned about the gross violations they were committing. My boy was told "nice, you want to make everyone sick" by the hall monitor. He was told by the vice principal that "I don't have time for that shit" when my son asked if she wanted to call me to verify if he was telling the truth about his exemption. He was told "you don't have a real exemption" because apparently that's what the VP told all the teachers, according to another teacher. He was shamed by students in the hall and on social media, and as much as I hold the school responsible for the division that was created, I know that this all stems from the fear the government and the media have brainwashed into people. I trust Nuremberg 2.0 is coming soon, and those who were responsible for creating Public Health Order Policies will be held accountable for what they are doing to humanity, and more importantly, to our kids. I am happy to say that the letter we provided had the school stand down on their harassment, even though they pushed to have Keaton come through his own door in class and move his desk away from his group in his cohort. We continue to push back and say "no" every time they discriminate against him. I am beyond grateful that my son is strong enough to stand his ground and stand up for his rights. He's a lion in my eyes who isn't cowering to authority, and this mama bear couldn't be prouder. One day I hope to have the school teaching the Charter of Rights and Freedoms, as it seems nobody knows when they're violating someone's rights or even when they are being violated against. Know your rights, protect your rights, or lose your rights has become my new motto.

As for my girl, she is boots-on-the-ground educating every business that tries to force her to wear a mask. She'll go right to the top and make sure the managers and owners know their employees are violating her rights, and they need to read page four of the PHO, which clearly states that exemptions do not apply to the mandates and must be taken at their word. For a girl who should have been spending her nineteenth year at night clubs and meeting new friends at university, she has spent most of her time alone, doing online classes, or hanging out with my husband and me on weekends. None of her friends are comfortable to come around anymore. COVID-19 has robbed her, and many other teens and young adults, of what should be some of the most memorable times of their lives. I don't understand why so many are blind to the inflated suicide, depression, and overdoses compared to actual Covid deaths. My kids have been my driving force to give me the strength to stand up. I have had to completely release all attachments to perfectionism and ego to speak out about this, as God knows most of my original friends and family think I am bat-shit crazy now. In the meantime, I love them from afar and keep fighting, educating, and advocating for truth anyway I can. I hope I can wake up the ones who mean the most before they give up all of their freedom or sign up for the experimental vaccine.

When COVID-19 first started to buzz in February 2020, the first thing I said was, "Mark my words, this is about a vaccine." Within a few weeks I was uncontrollably researching down the deepest darkest rabbit holes of government corruption. My eyes were wide open, but there was clearly a lot more at hand than just a pharmaceutical money grab. I found myself sharing information like crazy with a small handful of woke friends, which then led to getting brave enough to post the content online – but not until I had my little online army cushion my posts with comments of support in hopes of warding off the nay-sayers. Over the next few months, my Facebook posts were waking up many and also pissing many off. It seemed for every important person I lost I gained many more in followers wanting to see and use my content to wake up their own family and friends.

When social media advocacy no longer seemed to be enough, I had a calling to find like-minded thinkers in the flesh. Never in my life had I been to a protest, but here I was on Mother's Day, not only showing up, but scared as all hell and vibrating to speak out to the crowd. My friend, Brandi, said, "I can see you running one of these one day," and I was like, "Hell no! Are you kidding?" And then September rolled around, and with a handful of protests under my belt, I found myself volunteering to bring forward some of the most influential doctors and scientists of our time. With my mom's connections in the film industry, my friend Nia Peeples had offered to help me unite with the likes of Dr. Rashid Buttar, Del Bigtree, Robert Scott Bell, and Mikki Willis. I had other friends who were connecting me to David and Gareth Icke, David Avocado Wolfe, and Judy Mikovits, and before you know it, I had the honour of live streaming and introducing most of these amazing freedom fighting experts to thousands at the Vancouver Art Gallery in October. To step on stage was both terrifying and exhilarating, but shying away from the news and all the bad publicity leading up to the event was never an option. At this point, no matter how crazy I may come across to others, I don't think I could shut up if I tried! Once you wake up to the corruption, the easier it is to see through it, which just fuels me more to document, record, research, and reveal the truth about *everything* our corrupt government is taking part in. I won't stand down until they do.

Despite the disconnected relationships, the media calling our Freedom Rallies "anti-mask" events held by Neo Nazi's, fascists, bigots, and white supremacists and the endless volunteer hours invested into making a difference; the silver lining in this has been connecting with some of the most beautiful, heart-centred, egoless, hard-working, selfless people I have ever met in my life. Those who weren't in this for the right reasons have self-destructed and removed themselves from being part of this very important mission. Those who are in it for the right reasons are uniting and supporting each other any way they can.

After the October rally, my dear friend, Alicia Johnson, and I co-founded The Freedom Rally World Organization. We collaborated to support other leaders in the movement that had already been making waves for months. Our goal was to unite these groups under a banner called The Freedom Rally World Family, where we would all support and have input into upcoming events. Month after month we have been pulling off extraordinary protests featuring phenomenal global activists and experts in the medical industry. By far, my favourite event will always be throwing the biggest party in North America on New Year's Eve, where the masked and unmasked of all cultures danced the night away. It was a resistance to remember! We will oppose government orders and will celebrate the new year. And boy did we celebrate! If you missed this, you may want to consider coming next year, just sayin'. The media had a frenzy with us, calling us selfish, narcissistic super spreaders, but it's like water off your back when you know you have good people at your side. We are all just trying to show the world we have nothing to fear but fear itself.

Admittedly, being called selfish is probably one of the hardest insults to hear when so many of us are putting everything on the line to help humanity. That's why I was beyond excited when my freedom fighter sister, Amanda Forbes, reached out to see if I would like to be part of a project she and her friend Tania the Herbalist were going to venture out on. Only I couldn't imagine doing anything that didn't include Alicia, and I am so grateful that Tania and Amanda were totally on board with embracing us both to start the first ever online resistance called the Freedom for Truth Conference. Finally, we found a way for Canadians to come together, listen to speakers, learn, and not have to worry about losing their job for simply showing up. Furthermore, people's numbers will count for something as we are compiling a meta-analysis that will be submitted to the government on every level, along with polls telling what Canadians *really* want when it comes to lockdown measures, mandates, and vaccines. God knows the data pulled together by the mainstream media can't be trusted. The beauty of this platform is that people who wouldn't typically show up at a rally are showing up online. Some because this takes the risk out of losing their job and some out of sheer curiosity to see what this is all about. Either way, it's a win-win.

Our first conference featured Dr. Judy Mikovits, constitutional lawyer Rocco Galati, and Dr. Carrie Madej. Our platform was capped at a whopping 350 people despite the fact we had paid to house 10,000, and we had over 6,000 people trying to access the conference. We were told this was epic for a first go. #censorshipisreal. Note to self, no more playing in Bill Gates' backyard, aka MS Teams. Now we will pivot onto a new platform, and our next event is going to be even better!

If there's one person who knows how hard I've worked and how much I have put on the line, it would be my hubby, Chris, who I have been with for almost twenty-nine years. I honestly wouldn't be able to do half of what I am doing without his, or my kids', support. Undoubtedly, activism comes in many different forms, and I'd like to give a big shout out to all the spouses and kids who are supporting their crazy-ass activist family members because so much of this wouldn't happen without them being on board. It must seem that no sooner do I get one thing off my plate, on comes another project that I just can't stay away from. I am so grateful they have got my back. Please know the three of you are always my priority and are at the forefront of all my actions, and I can't thank you enough for your support and patience. We have gone through a lot to come together as a family over the past couple of years, and I promise we will be on a beach, together again, soon.

This has been a crazy year of intensive learning. It has been bittersweet, and every day I pray others wake up to the insanity in hopes the relationships that have been put on hold are able to come back together again soon. I have so much to be grateful for, especially to those who lovingly stand by me, to those who lifted or pulled me up into leadership, and to those who just shared their gratitude toward the work I have done so far. Sure, ignorance is bliss, but knowledge is power, and I wouldn't go back to ignorance for all the wealth in the world.
So, what does "For many are called, but few are chosen" actually mean? Like many, I was energetically invited to

step into something I felt extremely called to do. To be chosen is to have accepted the invite, which I continue to do each time a new door opens. I encourage everyone to listen to the voice of God inside you that is calling you to do what you came here to do; trust you will get the support you need to see it through. We are all called. Do yourself, and this world, a favour and RSVP. You are needed now more than ever!

About Danielle Elise Pistilli:

As an educator and expert in the field of energy medicine and colour therapy, Danielle Pistilli was a late bloomer to the world of advocacy. Danielle was born and raised in North Vancouver by a single mother from the age of eleven. As the oldest sibling of two, she grew up with a fair share of responsibility and adopted a take-charge kind of personality, which undoubtedly helped prepare her for what the world had in store for her in 2020. Never in a million years did she expect to be stepping into the kind of advocacy work she finds herself embedded in today, especially with a full-time job, an ill mother who is now living with her, two children, a dog, and a husband she has been with since she was eighteen years old.

Functioning on minimal sleep, Danielle is a work horse when it comes to seeing through all the projects she is working on, including co-organizing Freedom Rallies in Vancouver under the Freedom Rally World banner or online through The Freedom for Truth Resistance Conferences with The Freedom Organization team. There is no question that Dani is standing on the right side of history. She is clearly a natural born truth seeker, freedom fighter, and leader and is relentless in her pursuit of exposing government corruption and waking up her corner of the world. Her chapter is dedicated to the long line of strong women who helped to make her who she is today.

To download a copy of the letter to unmask your child, or for updates on The Freedom for Truth Conferences, go to www.thefreedomorg.ca or follow us on Facebook, Instagram, Twitter, or Telegram under The Freedom Organization.

For information on rallies around the world, go to www.freedomrally.world or follow us on Facebook, Instagram, or Telegram under Freedom Rally World.

Chapter Thirteen

Standing Out From The Crowd

By Caitlyn Richer

I never really thought of myself as an activist, but in the year 2020 my vision became much clearer – pun intended. I became much more self-aware and conscious of how I am different. It truly has been eye-opening.

I spent many years playing the "conform" game because I was never really taught autonomy. In this world, we are rarely encouraged to be different. The world would like to fit us in a box and teach us to conform to the "norm." Do not dare to think differently. There is only a small margin for individuality, and the moment you do think differently, you are soon harshly labeled weird, crazy, racist, anti vaxxer, anti-science, and likely a conspiracy theorist. But who decides what the "norm" is? From what do we base truth? Are you brave enough to ask these questions?

In my younger years, teens, and early adulthood, I suffered from many common health complications. I never felt well, and I was sick all the time. I exhausted all the medical system could offer, and after many long years, I decided to take my health in my own hands. In 2012, I saw a local naturopath and worked extremely hard to restore my health. The transformation happened so fast; I could hardly believe it. Within six weeks, almost all my symptoms were gone or improved by about 80%. This experience set me ablaze. I always knew I was different than most people growing up, but it was this moment I truly began to question everything we are taught. I accepted that most of what is mainstream is the very last thing we should be doing. I began to see the world differently, and a warrior was born within me. I wanted to teach people the things that could empower them and truly set them on fire – like I was. After all, no one will take care of you better than you can take care of yourself.

At the time, I was studying massage therapy, so natural health tied in perfectly with everything I was learning. Not long after I graduated, I grew the courage to quit my job and went fully self- employed. That is the way I like things. Sure, it was unpredictable and took time to build up, but I enjoy my freedom far too much not to be self-employed. Although natural health was the forefront of my passion, I was also interested in many topics within the "truth" community. I've spent a lot of time investigating various topics and theories - seeking to understand our world. The most important thing we can do for ourselves is take the time to investigate and form our own independent opinions separate from the voice of others and the indoctrination of our modern society. It is crucial to be presented with unbiased facts from all sides to allow us to make the best-informed decision we can for ourselves and our families. During this time, I also became acquainted with my spirituality, which really helped me to understand the events unfolding in the world. I believe our spirit is hard-wired for the truth from our Creator. If we honestly seek with an open heart, the door shall be open to us. (Matthew 7:7-8)

Standing Out From The Crowd

I wish it were as simple as it sounds, but unfortunately, this is not what we are currently experiencing. Massive censorship platforms have been developed by Big Tech to control free speech and the flow of information. It has become increasingly difficult to find or share any alternative views. We have entered a cancel culture that shuts down anyone who dares to share opposing views. This is not new to me, obviously, since I've spent the last eight years researching "conspiracy theories" and have seen tons of censorship and persecution of the "truth community."

Whilst the pandemic first began, I thought it was very odd right from day one. Call it discernment, I'm really not sure, but my first thought was a global pandemic was declared very prematurely. Cancelling major sporting events, Hollywood, and Disneyland when there were very little active cases? Hmmm. This was the first sign to me that something was odd. Of course, at the time, I really didn't know how this was going to unfold or if there was a true threat to my health on its way, so I watched to see. Only two weeks into the theatrics, I was sure we were being duped when I witnessed fake footage on every major news outlet being used to perpetuate fear.

Right then and there, the fire raged inside me, and I began speaking out against the narrative. I ignored any kind of stay-at-home order and exercised my fundamental rights to life and liberty. My son and I continued our outdoor adventures and enjoyed the beautiful spring weather. I had many people messaging me to ask what my thoughts were, and together we built a support community. In July, mandatory masking was implemented in our area. Immediately I investigated the exemptions and refused to ever mask myself or my son. I remember standing in Walmart, it was packed with people, and of several hundred people standing around waiting to check-out, I was the only one unmasked. I felt like every eye was on me and my stomach knotted. But then I felt a calmness come over me and a voice say, "It takes courage to stand out from the crowd. I made you this way." I decided then that I would continue to be brave. I would honor myself above the opinion of others. I refused to comply simply for comfort and conformity. I guess I had previous experience self-advocating, so this came naturally to me to honor my medical rights. I had done a lot of research on vaccines and the pharmaceutical industry prior to having my son, so I decided on an all-natural pregnancy and declined many of the modern tests and protocols. Luckily, I was not met with any resistance during this process.

In September 2020, I came across Susan Standfield on Facebook. She was living out west in BC and sharing daily videos about the pandemic and our human rights. I loved that she was empowering people to self-advocate and educating others, like I was. But she had so much more experience as an activist than I did. I learned a lot from her, and in October she called on women from all over the world to participate in civil disobedience, protests, or whatever you were comfortable with. Her passion was met with mine, and I decided it was my turn to make my move since nothing was happening in my community of Cornwall, Ontario. I decided to *be* bold and held the first "Cornwall March for Freedom" protest on October 24th, 2020 (seven months into the pandemic). I was surprised at how simple it was and how good it felt to take a stand. We had an overwhelming amount of people willing to help out with printing and other costs, and we even held a fundraiser to support ten local families through this difficult Christmas season. We had five local protests in total, and I was given a summons (charges) under the Reopening Ontario Act as an organizer – a challenge I was willing to accept for our freedoms. Of course, I am afraid the system might not act equitably and there may be consequences; however, I am far more afraid of what it means if we do not resist and fight for our fundamental freedoms. The biggest blessing in organizing a protest group was meeting so many like-minded people who are eager to learn. I am now surrounded by "woke folks." We have helped each other, supported one another, empowered one another, and taught each other what self-advocacy looks like – no one can advocate for you, it is something you must learn for yourself. I also started helping to distribute "nomorelockdowns.ca" signs around my community and surrounding area, as well as Druthers Newspapers, which are an alternative news source that is publicly funded and not bought out to control the narrative.

I, like everyone else, can have some pretty hard days. I have learned to listen to my body and mind. I have developed strong self-care routines to keep me going and mentally focused. This can look different for each of us, but my go-to things consist of: breathing exercises, listening to violin covers, reading, gardening, and having a nice hot bath/sitting in the sauna. It is also equally important to build yourself a strong community of support, even if it's virtually. I know many people are not so fortunate to have many like-minded friends, but thankfully social media can connect us world-wide with other like-minded folks who can become a support network. It has also become a huge source of alternative news and research. We can now access studies being done across the world within seconds of it being published online.

The Brave: Courage During COVID in Canada

I believe some people have been supernaturally gifted by God. Their eyes are open, but some lack the courage to speak the truth. *Dare to speak the truth.* You will come across many rejections, but dust your feet off and move forward anyway. In a world where we cannot be too sure of anything, one thing I am certain of is the effect we can have on others, individually, by stepping into our purpose and making ripples. We have a lot to learn of ourselves, and its time humanity discovers its true potential and purpose. But first, we must uncover the truth. This requires courage and curiosity. Esther 4:14 says, "Perhaps you were created for such a time as this."

Being brave can look like many things, but it starts with the courage to investigate followed by learning how to say NO to the things that do not feel authentic to you. Some use social media to share with others, some create a podcast or funny content, some create music or rap, some host small social groups in civil disobedience, some simply lead by example and empower others to be brave.

Whatever is the most authentic to you will work.

Everyone has their own unique voice to add and their own unique story to tell. Your story, when spoken aloud, could be the match that lights the flame for many others. Your courage will inspire others – I promise!

You are the light of the word.
Matthew 5:16

About Caitlyn Richer:

Caitlyn is a single mom to a wonderful and active boy. Her days consist of chaos, cooking, gardening, reading, researching, and creative art. Her natural health journey began in 2012 after a long battle with her own health issues. Exhausting the abilities of our modern medical system pushed her to seek out alternatives and her passion began. With this also came an intense spiritual adventure and journey of self-healing, which has given her the strength and courage to endure adversity. Being entrepreneurial-minded and having a strong passion for natural health led Caitlyn to recently build her passion into a business, educating and empowering others. Prior to that, she was a self-employed massage therapist adding various natural health modalities. She has always had a strong desire to help others.

Quoted from her social media: "I am a woman of many opinions and I often find myself freely sharing the matters on my heart. I hope to encourage others to bravely share their ideas and opinions – to freely express."

C A Marie Richer

#Thisisme

Chapter Fourteen

Faith Over Fear

By Tania Khazaal

Humble beginnings lead to bigger endings. It all started in Ottawa, the capital of Canada for me. I was born and raised in Ottawa with a Lebanese background. I had a drive for independence at a young age, and at fourteen, I started to work for the corporate world. From fast food stores, to studying business finance, obtaining my stock license, to becoming a top-selling insurance agent who was nationally recognized, this path led me to great success, expensive travels, and a wealth of money. Yet, it came with a great amount of grief.

 Working in the corporate world helped me obtain many skills I needed to build my own award-winning business; however, it came with many heartaches and pain. I watched my mother nearly succumb to the corrupt pharma industry that neglected her, over-medicated her, and treated her poorly. I battled health issues including chronic anxiety and endometriosis that was caused by a vaccine, and I watched my sister get taken advantage of by the health care system while she fought an auto-immune disease. Naturally I, through struggles of my own and feelings of helplessness, began to explore various things: self-help books, spirituality, neuroscience, and the power of natural healing in an effort to find balance and functionality in my life. After several difficult challenges, and the will to survive and thrive, I was led down a path of self-study and education of natural healing and plant medicine. As an unconventional thinker, I tapped into many parts of myself where I had triggered healing responses and took action to create the life I wanted. Becoming an activist and an herbalist goes hand in hand for me, bringing my heart and mind into equal rhythm.

My courage and will to stand up to oppression started when I was very young. From being punched in the face for standing up for someone being bullied, including myself, to taking leaps of faith and leaving very toxic situations and relationships that served me no good. Coming from humble beginnings and growing up in community living, I was forced to see some very sad and disturbing circumstances, such as a drive-by shooting at the age of seven, a family friend overdose at the age of fourteen, and my sister getting stabbed at a local fair when I was seventeen years old. Who would have thought these parts of my life would help shape my fierceness and my resistance to an oppressive and corrupted system as an adult?

These struggles and hardships helped form my character. I was bullied throughout elementary school and some high school for not only being a minority, but also for being different – wearing different clothes, listening to different music, and embodying my uniqueness. I started a new high school at age seventeen, which was my last year of high school. I knew no one, not a person. I ate lunch alone on many days, had very few friends, and heard a lot of nasty things said about me. I spent the year ignoring as much as possible and focused on getting good grades and graduating. I had almost finished the school year and faced a terrible encounter. A group of girls who bullied me throughout year happened to also be part of the yearbook committee. They wrote in big block letters "representin' the ghetto" as big as my name in all the yearbooks that were distributed to the school. Not one apology, no retraction or reprint of the yearbooks, and no repercussions. It was tough; it was hurtful. There is no denying that; however, I didn't let it change me. I remained true to myself, I stood up for myself, and grew a backbone to share this vulnerable story with others to help them understand that these "bullies" have unresolved issues of their own causing them to lash out at you. This experience helped me be brave, stand up to oppression, and to understand the lack of love in one's life creates anger, hate, and jealousy to others around them. It is not an indication of anything lacking in me. Through this struggle, it brought me more strength. What helped make me courageous is that I never forgot where I came from. No matter where I got and will go in life, I always appreciate where I came from because it made me who I am today.

I aim to live as selflessly as possible. I have put my life on the line to help others without thinking of the consequences it can bring me. I remember one day at a waterpark with a group of friends where I witnessed two young boys drowning in the wave pool. My friends thought they were play fighting because they were pushing each other underwater, but the moment I looked at them I knew they were fighting for their lives. Without hesitation, I shouted for the lifeguard and quickly swam toward them. By the time I got to them, one of the boys had started to pass out. I remember holding my breath, going under water, and pushing them both above me for them to gasp air. I lost consciousness shortly after and was pulled out of the water completely forgetting what had just happened a second ago. I will forever remember saving those boys' lives, even if that meant risking my own.

I would never have been able to live with myself knowing I didn't try to save them.

This bravery intertwined with my awakening to the corruption behind the medical industry. As previously mentioned, I saw my own family fight battles and be taken advantage of by the conventional system, but I also lived to see the oppression and bullying that can take place in a doctor's office. My family doctor bullied me when it came to my son and vaccinations. She tried to instill fear, she talked down to me and tried to intimidate me, including exposing and disclosing the financial incentives of vaccinations, indicating that if I choose to not go through with them, then I am not welcome for walk-ins. I stood strong and stood my ground to trust my instincts. This experience pushed me to do more research, which inevitably prepared me for the next steps of my life to fight the corruption in the medical and pharma industry.

A few years later, as the world moved into a "global pandemic," COVID-19 was introduced and helped shed light on the oppression but this time in a worldwide dynamic. It showed the true colours of many around me. People I admired, looked up to and loved, showed themselves to be cowards, quickly giving away my liberties for their false sense of safety and security. It showed how quickly people will turn aggressive on one another, create a civil war, and label individuals a certain term for not following the common narrative. It also shed light on the ability to control humans through years of predictive programming, manipulating thought processes, including influencing the masses to forget all other causes of death and primarily focus on COVID-19.

The Brave: Courage During COVID in Canada

I had a childhood friend overdose intentionally, I watched my mom overmedicate because of a surgery that was cancelled for months while she screamed of pain daily, and I witnessed humanity demonize me and others for not complying against unlawful mandates that are more dangerous than the virus. Within two weeks of flattening the curve, I quickly learned the control of society that was happening, the manipulation of numbers and cases, and the inflated deaths where one death was counted as two or more deaths. I strongly believe that this "pandemic" was an initiated problem, to initiate the solution of a vaccine. This is not any vaccine humans have ever seen before. This is synthetic mRNA that has never been tested on humans. This is an injection with horrific side effects that resulted in the last decade of animal testing that was done. This is a global control system, turning humanity into technological beings, losing their empathy, their natural instincts, their free will, and their soul.

I knew early on I couldn't and wouldn't be complacent to "rules" that went against my innate human nature and instincts. I practiced and promoted civil disobedience by not wearing a mask, seeing my family and friends whenever I desired, and by sharing public videos to help spread the truth, the corruption, and the fraud that was happening behind this pandemic. As a mom and business owner, I am putting my life on the line every day to speak and spread the truth, living fearless of the consequences as I truly believe that if God is on my side, who can be against me? He is the ultimate of planners, and as long as I fight the good fight, I have nothing to fear. Through my struggles, I found my strength that helped shape this mindset of "facing oppression without fear." I always tell myself it is either a lesson or a blessing, and every obstacle and triumph is bringing me closer to that greater purpose.

At the beginning of COVID-19, many people gravitated toward me because I was one of the very few speaking out against the narrative and the measures. I asked questions, I used critical thinking, and I opposed the draconian and harmful measures. The need for a leader and guidance among the people was evident. I felt compelled to take that lead, to follow God's purpose for me on this journey, and to be the brave wolf among the herd of sheep that would help initiate the movement to sovereignty. This path naturally led me to becoming a freedom fighter, creating a website sharing our rights, providing resources to high quality documents and studies provided by scientists, epidemiologists, and experts all over the world, and educating on the dangers of masks, isolation, social distancing, and vaccines.

We all have that courage inside of us, but unfortunately many have a hard time bringing it out because of fear of confrontation, not being liked, or getting ridiculed. This tends to stem from the lack of healing from past experiences, trauma, and beliefs. I, with lots of inner work, tapped into my healing responses and broke free of that fear, broke free of past beliefs, and took a leap of faith in situations that many wouldn't have had the courage to do. Just to give an example, at the age of twenty-six, I was very unhappy, drowning in debt, in a toxic relationship, had a miserable job, and living with my best friend at the time who had a household full of drama of her own. I looked up to God and I spoke to Him and told him, "My way isn't working; I need your help. I need you to guide me, bring me on my path of purpose, and show me the way." I woke up one morning with renowned strength. That week I broke up with my partner, quit my job without having another job, and I moved back into my parents' house all within a matter of a couple days.

I cried and felt like a failure. I made that hard decision to take a leap of faith and trust God 100% to heal, guide, and help me find my destined path. And He did! I found a job that forever changed my life, I found a partner who is on the same deep wavelength as me, and the rest became history. This is the leap of faith and courage that many are afraid to take but don't recognize how liberating and empowering it truly is. If everyone tapped into their soul and intuition, they would see and hear their inner voice guide them to their destiny and to live fearlessly. When you stand up for yourself, when you stand up for your God given rights, you not only feel empowered, but you find your tribe of like-minded people. You connect with life, earth, nature, and humans on a deeper level and quickly recognize how much bigger we are then the box the media and the government has put us in.

The best advice I can give is to have faith over fear. Find your faith in a society that has become so disconnected from God, and reconnect with your heart and soul. Eliminate the processed foods, the GMOs, the fluoridated water, anything that depletes your pineal gland and microbiome. Eat and drink your plants, sun gaze, hug as much as possible, and connect with others. This is the mind, body, and spiritual connection you need to hear your inner voice. Live fearlessly! Teach your children and future generations what it means to be brave, because you don't want to look back one day wishing you had been braver and done more.

I believe the uprising is here. The strong, the awoken, the courageous have come together, banded an allegiance, and formed an international tribe to fight this battle. Once you are awake, you don't go back to sleep. The harder they

Faith Over Fear

push, the harder we push back. The more they censor, the louder we get. The more they take, the more we resist.

I am grateful God chose me along with many others to fulfill our duty to humanity!

"Keep your faith high and your fear low."
By: Tania Khazaal (Tania The Herbalist)

About Tania Khazaal:

Tania is a practicing herbalist with an award-winning business offering organic products, eBooks, and training courses. Coming from the corporate world, Tania was making well over six figures but hit rock bottom when she, her mother, and sister nearly succumbed to the pharma industry. She used this breaking point to find her passion in natural healing, speak up about the corruption behind big pharma, and has a life motto of "facing oppression without fear." She educates, coaches, and shares her knowledge with the public on healthy habits, healing through herbs, overcoming anxiety, facing oppression, and empowering others to have faith over fear. Tania is someone who went from being bullied throughout life, filled with anxiety, to building a successful business and using her voice to help people overcome the oppressive behavior of others.

Contact Information:
Email: taniatheherbalist@protonmail.com
Telegram: https://t.me/taniatheherbalist
Instagram: @taniatheherbalist
Facebook: Tania The Herbalist & Coach (facebook.com)
Twitter: @taniatheherblst

Chapter Fifteen

Fuel Purpose

By Dr. Dena G. Churchill

Brave. The only image I can drum up with the word brave is the movie *Braveheart*. The 1995 American film directed by Mel Gibson, who portrays a thirteenth century Scottish warrior, William Wallace. Wallace ultimately gets captured and taken to the gallows, where his last words, after he has been tortured and before he's decapitated, are those of inspiration as he bellows the word "Freedom!" into the wind on his last breath.

When Lani asked me to participate in this book, I tried to turn down the opportunity as the word brave didn't really resonant with me. Brave is going to war, fighting, and risking your life for people whom you may never meet, having your guts removed with a meat hook on a public stage and coming to an untimely death for your efforts. Informing police, politicians, and media about the scam of covid and refusing to wear a mask is simply sharing truth. Is sharing truth brave?

"Is sharing truth brave?" If I qualify speaking truth as "brave," then the opposite must also be true. Silence is "cowardly." Some spiritual masters would call silence wisdom, so herein, we'd have a cognitive dilemma. This duality sets the stage for separation of our humanity. Brave could provide mirror mimicry, or it could disconnect others from their own magnificence. There are times when I am courageous and there are times when I am cowardly, so in this chapter I would like to share both. I pray in this truth you see your reflection, attach to your own brilliance, as we meet heart to heart.

There were times when speaking truth had some gut wrenching consequences, both on a local Halifax platform and a Canadian stage. CBC titles of "Doctor loses chiropractic license" and "Chiropractor pays a 100K fine and is labelled as delusional and incompetent" were painful. Being mocked in professional hearings and ordered to see a psychologist caused me, at times, to doubt my own sanity. I didn't die, but maybe it counts as "brave" to watch your friends die for sharing the same vaccine dangers and still choosing to speak. Many holistic doctors came to untimely deaths for revealing the disease, injury, and deaths caused by vaccines. Most recently, two dear friends, Sallie Elkordy (vaccine-free world) and Brandy Vaughan (learntherisk.org), came to a sudden demise after having a few warnings to keep quiet by the pharmaceutical mafia. Dr. Rebecca Carly, reformed natural health medical doctor, wore a delusional label when it was leaked that she healed 5,000 autism cases. To overcome these personal fears and doubts, I had to connect to a higher purpose and pray: "God, where you guide, I trust you will provide. Protect my family, and if there is consequence to my actions, let it fall upon me." There are many times I'd thought about throwing in the towel and giving up ... but then a voice arrived to remind me of this sacred duty, and I couldn't say "no" to God.

The pain of witnessing neurological damage to a healthy baby after vaccine injections was a silent heartache that fuelled a different purpose. However, at times it didn't feel courageous when I was curled up in a ball with the covers over my head, crying, mourning the loss of our family home, my chiropractic practise, reputation, and economic stability. I didn't feel brave when I was depressed, living in my stepfathers basement with nothing but the clothes on my back and a few boxes of books. After giving up my chiropractic license and clinical practice, I was deflated and defeated and felt I wasn't making any difference. By the time Covid came around, I had already been in battle for two years, and I was at an all-time low. When news spread that the outbreaks of measles, mumps, and polio were from the vaccine strand of the "virus," the global muppets had to come up with a new fearful "boogie-man" virus to sell the vaccine agenda. The FDA approved the Ebola "vaccine" in November 2019, so it looked as though they were preparing for an Ebola outbreak. But maybe Ebola would have looked too obvious, so the Coronavirus, being a new imposter, created more fear. The Covid scam gave me enough anger (fear turned inside out) to have a renewed sense of purpose and energy. I was waiting for an outbreak, so it didn't surprise me, but the extent to which they played out this global lie was shocking! I became so busy digging into the research to reveal the truth of the scam that I forgot to be depressed. Stepping outside of my own small perspective of self-pity and attaching to a higher brain function of world service is a great empowerment tool. Inspired action takes you out of the amygdala (emotional centre) into poised, powerful, and purposeful action. Fear can paralyze you, but when you can turn it into fuel, you become an unconquerable breed.

In April 2020, sitting in my car at Costco with steam coming out my nose and fire on my breath, the tales of toilet paper brain-washing, muzzle masks, and the medical mafia monopoly of the media rolled off my tongue. The global plan to enslave every man, woman, and child wasn't a new concept. John F Kennedy exposed this in a speech in 1962, two weeks before he was taken out of commission. The 300,000+ views on that particular Facebook video (https://www.bitchute.com/video/tEFSMnbUlVjl/) initially gave me a spark of hope that more and more were waking up to the greater agenda. The spark dimmed with a further ten months of tyranny and the masked masses catering to the agenda. The disappointment with our current government inspired me to other platforms.

On Sept 18th, 2020, I and twenty-eight others founded the Atlantic Common Law Assembly as a way to awaken people to their natural born rights and freedoms. My spell as ACLA convener lasted for five months until I burned myself out with administrative work, eating up time and energy from writing and speaking. The four weekly zoom meetings and the protests at city halls, presentations to legislatures, demonstrations at farmers markets, visits to the Department of Education and political offices were good public education tools, but the stars aligned and the winter solstice hit me with a bang. On December 21st, 2020, at the Great Cosmic Conjunct, I had a vision. I could see being in that particular leadership position allowed others to depend on me instead of depending on themselves. I could see how the Covid challenges were a gift. The COVID-19 scam was the culmination of a hundred-year-old plot of enslavement, and the current environment was the festering wound of the toxins coming to the surface. For the first time in thousands of years, the masses were being given an opportunity to take back their power. My heart opened with this revelation, and love and gratitude leaked from my eyes. I had been forgetting a foundational principle in our human existence that *pain* is a *great teacher*. The greatest reset.

Fuel Purpose

People act with apparent courage because the result of not acting is more painful. They overcome their individual fears to attach to a higher purpose. Inspiration, like wisdom as Confucius says, can be reflected or imitated, but pain is the best bittersweet kick-in-the-ass. Businesses have a choice to drown in government policy or swim in their own authority. Police officers have a choice to follow a corrupt corporate agenda or serve the people. Politicians who put in the mandates have a choice to serve their constituents or be held liable for their damages. In this role of legislative influencer, every member of the Legislative Assembly in four different provinces and the members of Parliament, police, and media in Nova Scotia were sent all the scientific information of mask dangers, the PCR test fraud, and the scam of Covid. The strategies of thanking them for their honorable service while threatening personal liability for death or injury caused by their recommended restriction didn't seem to be making a difference. On March 5th, 2021, I sent a Freedom of Information request to the Nova Scotia government. Without the government reply, proving the SARS CoV2 genetic material actually causes COVID-19 symptoms and proving all the measures of masks, distancing, and "vaccines" are safe and effective, they fall into a commercial default position and are liable for damages. At the time I am writing this, March 25th, 2021, it has been seventeen days without a government reply. However, I am hopeful that in this inaction others see the incongruence, awaken, and align to their power.

Holding our own vibration and intention at a higher level creates a new reality as we become the creator. Similar to the law of attraction, we first have to be it and feel it to see it. A new focus was to "be the change" and hold a space for that transformation. Instead of protesting in the parking lots of the big box stores, I found greater purpose in boycotting these globalist businesses and supporting our own local organic farmers and craftspeople. The business that didn't allow me to enter without a mask, I moved from the human rights commission complaint file to my email education database for regular updates. Instead of feeling ostracized and threatened because I was different, I began to see myself as a Goddess who had risen above the folly of mortal men with an obligation to teach those who had not yet owned these credentials. IKEA, Sobeys, Smitty's, Health Food Store, Home Hardware, Halifax Shopping Centre, Dollar Stores, hairdressers estheticians, massage therapists, chiropractors, and many other restaurants allowed me full breathing service. I would promote and thank these businesses by giving them repeat business and referring them to others. I made it a point to remember their names, too, and left mask exemption cards for them that I had printed through Rebel News. Love and kindness is a universal vibration, a mutual channel of communication. I had a front row seat with all the oxygen I could breathe because I chose it and didn't consent to anything less. Wayne Dyer used to say, "You have to teach people how you wish to be treated." How and what are you teaching? Could this problem of consenting to tyranny be, at a fundamental level, low self-esteem, lack of confidence, and not owning your own authority?

COVID-19 didn't really change life for me too much, as I had already surrendered my government regulated profession after twenty-two amazing years. Covid (certification of vaccine identification) felt like the final finale of a century-long tyrannical play. The outlandish restrictions lifted the veil so many more could see the hidden truths. I was almost hoping for a poster or video with Dr. Tam demonstrating her recommendations. It would have been striking advertising for the play to see her wearing a three-ply mask stuck to a "glory hole!" Heheehe. Breathing freely, working your business, and removing yourself from places where you are being abused is a healthy practise.

"I can't wear a mask; it reduces my oxygen and suppresses my immune system."

"If I can't shop here and breathe freely, then I am reporting you to the human rights commission and taking my business elsewhere."

"Are you medically qualified to ask me to wear a mask or take my temperature?"

"Are you willing to take personal liability for any death or damages this may cause to me or my family?"

"If there are more deaths from the Covid shot than from the apparent "virus," is this really "health care" or is it genocide?"

"I do not consent. Read the science and you won't either."

This corona "virus" – dead bits of genetic material – was never Koch postulated isolated. The PCR test is at best inaccurate. At the worst, it is introducing nanotechnology to make you ill and the pandemic is fake. There have been no more deaths from this crazy cold than any flu in any other year. Articles entitled "Masked Truths" (https://www.healthtruth.blog/blog/masked-truths) and "Spectrums of Energy" (https://www.healthtruth.blog/blog/spectrums-of-energy) discuss how the fifth generation of cellular technology is an actor on a breathless stage and how COVID is the smokescreen for the 2030 agenda. The plandemic was to reduce and control our population, to make us financially dependent on government, and to introduce humans into the smart grid using the nanotechnology. As Dr. David Martin reports, the COVID shot cannot be legally defined a "vaccine," as there is nothing in it to prevent transmission or to protect you against Covid symptoms. It is a medical device and a bioweapon. The 1972 mandate of the WHO to kill using vaccines was a dead giveaway to their intention.

Gandhi says when the government becomes lawless and corrupt then it is our sacred duty to resist and change the paradigm. But the concept of "civil disobedience" is still playing in a lower realm of understanding where power, fear, and force are used to move and manipulate. You must know the details but then rise above it to "divine alignment" to change it. You can't change the matrix on the same dense frequencies in which it was created. Love holds a space for transformation. *Murder by Decree* details how Queen Lizzy, in combined operation with the Vatican, the British Crown, the Government of Canada, Catholic, Anglican, and United Churches killed over 60,000 indigenous children in the so-called residential school system. The government supported their forced vaccination, rape, and murder since 1874. If we can jump out of our legal/illegal perspective into a cosmic vision where God is our highest authority, then all other incomplete paradigms beneath disappear, and our influence is global. Seeing it as "disobedience" is like looking at the glass half empty. The full glass (the eye at the top of the pyramid) is seeing lawful truth, justice, love, and wisdom of divinity within you. At this level of consciousness, you surpass the lower realms of existence and create your own reality. Ask yourself what God would

Fuel Purpose

do, then do it. Some may see it as brave, some may see it as foolish, some may even call you delusional, but in this vibration, the voices on the outside are background harmony for your own love song as you master your own destiny. Natural love is a supernatural phenomenon.

Courage uses fear to fuel a purposeful path. You have a choice to fear the fire or become the flame. When you become the flame, you have everlasting life. When it is time to pass over into the next lifetime, you travel light, knowing you did the best with what you know, believe, and have. Humanity is a fatal condition, but love is an eternal legacy. Acting now with God as your highest authority, you become immortal. Speak truth. Share love. Be the change. William Wallace: "Run, and you'll live ... at least a while. And dying in your beds, many years from now, would you be willing to trade all the days, from this day to that, for one chance – just one chance – to come back here and tell our enemies that they may take our lives, but they'll never take our freedom!"

Live enslaved or die free!

About Dr. Dena G. Churchill:

Dr. Dena Churchill is an international speaker, author, and innovator in women's health and wellness. She is known for her ability to deeply connect with audiences through clarity, wisdom, and humour. With a humble confidence, she draws on a wealth of real-life experiences to help you "Envision and Achieve Your Best" in a way that is both entertaining and informative. Dr. Dena combines the ageless wisdom of the mind, body, spirit balance, integrating her studies in psychology, astrology, biology, nutrition, neurology, chiropractic, and spirituality to provide you with fresh ideas in healing and transformation. She is the author of the book entitled *Divinity in Divorce*; contributing author to *Pearls of Wisdom- Pure and Powerful*, and *The Thought That Changed Your Life Forever*. Publicly, she aspires to be a legislative influencer. Privately, she is a health coach of quantum healing medical astrology. In January 2019, after twenty-two years in private family practise, Dr. Dena surrendered her chiropractic license to avoid further persecution in suspension and fines for speaking about the dangers of vaccines and vaccine injuries.

Blog: https://www.healthtruth.blog/
Youtube: Dr. Dena Churchill
Facebook: DrDenaC

Fuel Purpose

Instagram: dr.denachurchill
Bitchute: Dr. Dena Churchill
Twitter: dr.denachurchill

Dr. Dena G Churchill BSc., DC.
Innovator in Women's Health.
https://www.healthtruth.blog/

Chapter Sixteen

Spirit of Rebellion

By Mark Friesen

My rebellious spirit is not something that has been nurtured nor something I grew into. As far back as I can remember, I have stood against what I believed to be injustice. It's in my DNA. You can't even blame my parents; they worked hard to tamp down that aspect of my personality. Of course, I responded with more defiance. I remember when I was a youngster in high school. It was a Catholic high school, so I was regularly in defiance mode. In particular, there was a time when the school administration decided that boys shouldn't be allowed to wear shorts in school because they were "too revealing." Yet, the girls were still allowed to wear skirts. Naturally, the day the directive came into effect, I wore shorts. I was immediately kicked out of my first class. I walked home, proud of myself for taking a stand, yet nervous about how my parents would react. I thought they would have to support me; this directive was insane. Well, I was wrong. Mom, being a teacher herself, did not take my side. Unfortunately, this was not a hill for my dad to die on either, so no support from him. Back to school I went the next day. Wearing pants. But then, a few guys thought the way around this was to wear skirts. It's hot outside, we're hot, girls can wear skirts, why can't we? This was 1987. Boys wearing skirts was not "acceptable." If this was 2021, our plan would have worked, except the plan wouldn't be necessary. Anyway, the point is that I have come into his

Spirit of Rebellion

fight honestly. This rebel spirit has been part of me my whole life.

The rebel spirit was also joined by a strong sense of justice, a strong sense of right and wrong. Along with defying the establishment, I stood up to bullies. Not on my own behalf, as I never really had any trouble myself with bullies, but on behalf of other folks who fell prey to them. Understanding what made me tick, and knowing who I was and what I believed in, I decided in grade ten to become a corrections officer (prison guard). I was attracted to the job through family who were working at the local federal penitentiary. I found out fairly soon in my career that bullies weren't only wearing inmate uniforms but they were also in management, as well as in the union. I spent twenty-five years fighting bullies in prison, in management, and in the union at great expense to my career – but I maintained my integrity until the end. So to say the actions I have recently been a part of are in line with my personality would be an underestimation at best.

However, the battle we are in now is much more significant, in size and consequence. This situation we have all been thrust into has been in the planning for many years. During the last eighteen years I have been studying globalism, Agenda 21/2030/UN agendas, and more recently, the Great Reset. 9/11 was my wake up call. Such a significant event in so many people's lives. I needed to know what created the circumstances for 9/11 to happen. That's when my research began. It started with trying to understand Islamism and Islamic terrorism, and why people were drawn into that ideology. While learning a lot about that particular ideology, my research would inevitably always lead me to the UN and the globalist agenda. This agenda was created to centralize global governance at the UN. The agenda was created by a small group of elites through an organization called the Club of Rome in the late '60s, who conceptualized Agenda 21 and the sustainable development to deal with population control, world economies, and development through redistribution of wealth and centralization of global power. Over years of research and study, I became a quiet activist. Someone who would simply attempt to educate the people around me and on social media as to the nefarious agenda that is at play and has been at play for many years. My activism changed dramatically in the fall of 2018. I went from a relatively quiet activist to boots-on-the-ground educator and influencer. Given that the issue of globalism is very much a political one, I paid a lot of attention to what our national governments were doing, whether conservative or liberal. It became very clear that all parties had bought into globalism, signing UN agreements in this regard since 1992. It was clear that if we were going to oppose globalism, we would need to oppose the establishment governments in Canada. However, there was no option for many years and politically, I felt I was on a deserted island, politically homeless. Enter Maxime Bernier and the creation of the People's Party of Canada. Maxime created the party based on core values I could work with to help wake a nation to the globalist agenda. But that in itself proved to be a bit of a hill to climb. Many discussions with Max and party brass would be necessary to get even them to understand what the globalist agenda was and the enormous consequences that agenda had for our nation. Through that evolution it became clear that I had a home politically and helped build the party from the ground up.

During that process, another entity was created in Canada. The yellow vest movement. A movement that started in France due to higher fuel taxes being imposed on the French in the name of climate change. It wasn't long and that movement was embraced in Canada, citing two issues: the carbon tax and the migrant compact. I immediately joined that movement and held the first rally in Saskatoon with a few associates with whom I had met through the Peoples Party. My life as a true activist began at that moment. Using that platform, as well as the platform created by the People's Party, I began my mission. A mission to educate and inform as many people as possible about the UN agenda and the serious consequences it will have on our way of life, our culture, our economy, and our prosperity. Through my yellow vest association, I also assisted in organizing the United We Roll Convoy to Ottawa in early 2019. An action that, again, provided an opportunity to educate as many folks as possible as to the reality of globalism. Alongside my activities with the yellow vest movement and the convoy to Ottawa, I was also still involved in growing the People's Party, walking a tightrope between activities, as the yellow vest movement was apolitical. However, I still recognized that if we are going to wake a nation and stop the globalist agenda, politics would play a huge role in that. After a number of significant yellow vest rallies after the convoy, I pulled back from the yellow vest movement and focused my time and energy on the People's Party. It was at that time, spring of 2019, that I accepted an invitation to run as a candidate for the People's Party. Not because of a lifelong dream of being a politician; I never wanted to be a politician or ever thought I'd be one. I've never been a fan of politicians, especially the establishment politicians. But again, it was an opportunity to use a platform to educate and inform as many people as possible. Mission accomplished in that sense. The PPC did not do well in the polls; however, we were able to attract 300,000 people to vote for the PPC, in large part due to our stance against the globalist agenda and globalism.

During that campaign as a candidate, it became even more abundantly clear that the vast majority of the masses were woefully ill-informed and uneducated about the globalist agenda, globalism, and the sustainable development agenda. In November 2019, I decided to form an organization called the Forum for Canadian Sovereignty, modeled after European groups who were fighting for the survival of their respective nations. Again, as a way to educate the masses as to what globalism meant for the people. As we officially became a non-profit corporation, the only non-profit, non-government organization opposing globalism, Covid entered. Lockdowns came, freedoms were lost. We had to adjust our model of holding town hall speaking engagements across the country to becoming involved in and supporting protest groups and the freedom movement.

A few short months after the 2019 election, Covid-19 enters our lives. As with most folks, I was watching and listening to what was being promoted on the news. Nobody really knew much about what was going on and/or what it meant. But even in the original sense of panic established by the media, I was skeptical given the research I had done on the globalist agenda. To achieve the massively transformative goals of the sustainable development agenda, a huge shift in public perception and attitudes would have to be achieved. We saw this social engineering with the fear mongering of climate change. Using people's fears to change behaviours, up to and including acceptance of a carbon tax. That was done through fear. Fear that the world will end in twelve years. With that context, I was skeptical of the Covid alarm, however I was still watching and learning about what this thing was. Then the lockdowns started in mid-March 2020. I became more skeptical. Similar strategies were being employed from the UN and the World Health Organization as had been used with climate change by the UN and the IPCC. Very effective strategies to get the masses to comply and submit to transformative behavioural changes. Again, it is in context of this overall agenda one can easily understand the measures taken are in concert with the greater agenda. In late spring 2020, I was made aware of a protest group in downtown Saskatoon. It was time to join the movement once again! Not only to oppose the masking of our population and the measures yet to come, but to once again use the platform to educate and inform as many people as possible within the movement and collaterally to the masses. In my view, it wasn't about climate change. It still isn't. It isn't about a virus; it's all about controlling the populace, socially engineering the masses to be complicit and submissive.

During the period from the creation of the PPC, the yellow vest movement, the convoy to Ottawa, the political campaign, the Forum for Canadian Sovereignty, and the freedom rallies, I have managed to get a decent following on YouTube and other social media platforms – fighting censorship the whole way. Posting almost daily live streams with guests or alone for almost three years, I am able to use my platforms to educate, motivate, and inspire others to get involved with local rallies and big national ones. With the help of many, many great patriots, we were able to organize the Canada1st Freedom Rally in Ottawa on Canada Day 2020. I, and numerous other patriots, took a small convoy from western Canada to Ottawa. The second time convoying forty-four hours one way to get to the nation's capital; yet another piece to this amazing puzzle of waking a nation. Then in the fall of 2020, I was invited to speak and attend the mega rally in Vancouver, BC. Once again we formed a convoy from Saskatchewan, to Revelstoke, to Kelowna, and finally to Hope, BC, where we had a convoy of over one hundred vehicles drive the highway from Hope to Vancouver to attend the rally there.

In early 2021 we, as a forum, the forum for Canadian Sovereignty and the convergence of many great patriots, have decided to expand our reach. Instead of waiting for folks to come to our rallies for information and fellowship, we are taking the message to the people. We have asked people in their own communities to organize a group of people to attend an information session. Not publicly promoted, but as a "clandestine" or "secret" meeting at an undisclosed location, under the radar of authoritarian government officials and restrictions against gathering or assembling. A strategy achieving amazing success so far.

This life choice ... who am I kidding? It's not a choice; I have no choice. This is my calling. It is what I am meant to do. It hasn't come without consequences. My circle of friends has changed dramatically. It's not a bad thing but a reality nonetheless. Although I must say, a number of my old friends are right beside me, the list just got a 'lil smaller. But my circle is much larger now with new amazing friends. Patriot friends. Friends willing to sacrifice for our country and the values we cherish. I have received four $2800 tickets with two more on the way – well, maybe three on the way, given the success of the last protest. I have been shamed in the media across the country. Hit pieces have been written about me that don't include an ounce of truth but are made simply to cast me off in the eyes of the public. I have had my business attacked online, a business I depend on to employ my two sons and other employees. I depend on my business to provide for my family and their future. This battle I was born to fight comes with consequences, but those consequences pale in comparison to what it would be like if I had to look at myself in the mirror every day and had done nothing at all.

This is war we are in, and it is an information war, a cultural war, and a spiritual war. It is a world war. Our enemies want to destroy our nation, our values, and our prosperity. We must unite to achieve critical mass in order to defeat this enemy. We will only be able to unite in defense of everything we cherish if the people use their inherent power. The people will only be empowered through information. To this point, our enemy has used the media to lock down the particulars. However, we are busting through the media lockdown by getting the intelligence to the masses who are starving for information and begging to understand, even if they don't realize it. They don't know what they don't know. It's up to us, the awakened, to share the knowledge, give people the power they were born to have, and inspire them to join this fight to defeat the common enemy. We need to put aside our petty differences, our particular identities, and unite to defend the common values we all share: freedom, sovereignty, justice, equality under the law, and prosperity for all.

About Mark Friesen:

Mark was born and raised in Saskatchewan. He went to Catholic elementary & high school. He was heavily involved in sports growing up. He started his own career in corrections when he was nineteen and worked in a number of maximum security institutions both provincially and federally. He was exposed to the darkest side of life in that time, including incredible corruption in the bureaucracy. He spent most of his career fighting management and the unions over safety issues, and he's been fighting for justice his entire adult life. Mark managed to start his own business and turn it into an exit strategy while still working in federal corrections. After four years of working and running a business, he was able to retire from working for the man and work full time for himself.

When they say find something you love, do it, the money will come ... they were right. Mark hasn't looked back. He is married with three children, and since he had 'em young, they are all out on their own and he's not even fifty yet. While he waits patiently for grandkids, Mark cherishes freedom, individual freedom, and national freedom and sovereignty. Always have, always will, and will fight to the death to regain it if that's what it takes.

"You can't be brave without first being afraid." ~ Mark

Chapter Seventeen

Courage through the Darkness

By Amanda Moses

I was born in North Bay, Ontario, but moved to Cranbrook, British Columbia, at the age of five. I was privileged to have been raised there in a loving and tight-knit family. I moved back to Ontario as a young mother at the age of eighteen. I began a job at a telemarketing call center while going through school to be an LPN, where I met my husband to be. Not long into my schooling, I realized I was not meant for the highly demanding job of a nurse, and I decided to pursue my lifelong dream of being a wife, raising children, and starting a hobby farm in the countryside.

A year after my husband and I were married, we welcomed our first daughter, Chloe, into this world. It was with her that my whole world changed, and I became the person who I am today. When I had my first son as a young mother, I never questioned the advice of my family doctor. When he told me my son needed to be vaccinated, I listened without second thought. I would notice my son Westly would immediately get very ill after his vaccines and would need to be taken to the hospital because he would stop eating and drinking. He also had ear infections, tonsillitis, and breathing difficulties. I noticed a change in his behaviour and demeanor following his twelve month vaccines. He went from being a very happy child to being quiet, and he would get in a rage at the smallest thing.

Because of the experience with my son, my husband and I held off on vaccinating our daughter. She never had a single ear infection or needed antibiotics for anything. She never had a reason to see a doctor because she was so healthy and developing tremendously. A family member of ours (who is an RN) found out our daughter was seventeen months old and was never vaccinated. The person used guilt and fear on us, and against our better judgement, we conceded and had her vaccinated.

With our daughter not being vaccinated, the doctor recommended she have several all at once to catch her up. We physically restrained our terrified and screaming daughter while they gave her several shots in her arm and both legs. They said she would more than likely not feel well and told us to start giving her Tylenol.

That night, my daughter developed a very high fever and high-pitched scream like we have never heard before. It continued throughout the night. The next day, when she would try to get up and stand or walk, she would wobble and fall to the ground. She would plug her ears and scream and cry non-stop. We assumed she had developed an ear infection like my son, so we bought her in to the doctor. They gave her antibiotics for a supposed ear infection, and the doctor said she probably wasn't walking because her legs were sore from the vaccinations.

We expected our daughter's usual demeanor would come back as the antibiotics started working. About four to six months had passed, and our daughter was still constantly plugging her ears and crying, even though she had no ear infections. When we brought her back to the doctor to see why she was acting like this, he told us it was normal because vaccines stimulate the immune system. He said she needed another set of shots to catch her up.

The nurse came in with the vaccines, and I told her I didn't want to do it because of the serious and sudden changes I saw with the last set. She said to me, "Would you rather a sick kid or a dead kid?" Out of fear, I agreed again.

After that set of vaccines, what little was left of our daughter's previous personality was completely gone. She no longer maintained any eye contact. She lost all words and communication, and she would do nothing but self-harm, scream, cry, and aggressively plug her ears. We were devastated. When we showed our family doctor how much worse she had gotten, he said that for "reasons unknown" some children all of a sudden start showing signs of autism around this age. He referred her to a pediatrician to be diagnosed. She was later diagnosed to be more severe than 68% of children on the autism spectrum. The hardest day of our lives was hearing from the pediatrician that my previously perfect daughter would now need constant care for the duration for her life. He said I should start thinking about putting her in a home, as it's easier for them to adjust to living in a home when they are young. The hopes and dreams I had of my beautiful daughter growing up and getting to enjoy normal things people do, like going to prom, getting married, or having children, were no longer going to be in her future. It was all robbed from her by a product I was told would make her life better.

While our daughter was being diagnosed, we had our son Jacob. Because of the severity of Chloe's autism, she required several different therapies and interventions. We lived in a rural area that was an hour drive from her services, so financially it became too much to afford. We were offered help for travel through CAS, but they had to open a file in order to provide the services. When my daughter started the IBI service, we no longer needed help with the travel.

When I told them we no longer required their services and they can close our file, they told us that because our youngest son was not vaccinated, it can be considered neglect. They were going to hold off on closing the file until he was vaccinated, even though the file was not opened for a case of abuse or neglect in any way.

I was fearful of losing my child to CAS because of the misleading words the case worker said. So, I took my son in to be vaccinated. I had always thought the reason my daughter had such a serious reaction to her vaccines was because she had so many at once, so I only allowed for my son to receive one vaccine that day. They gave him the MMR.

Like our daughter, our son was also in perfect health and development. He never needed antibiotics prior to vaccines for anything. After the vaccine he received, he also broke out in a very high fever that was on and off for over a week. At the end of the week, he seemed to get weaker and sicker. My cousin had come to visit us, and my son took a sudden and dramatic turn for the worse. His breathing became very shallow, his lips started turning blue, and he was very lethargic. We began driving him the thirty minutes to the closest hospital, and on the way, my cousin noticed my son was having what looked like to him to be a seizure. When we arrived at the hospital, I noticed my son was talking funny and one side of his face looked droopy, like someone who had just had a stroke. Because of my son's face, the ER doctor told us it would be better to send him to the next better equipped hospital by ambulance.

At the hospital, I told the pediatrician on call what had happened. I mentioned that I felt it was a reaction to his vaccines, and that all my children had bad reactions after receiving them. She said, "Vaccines don't cause those reactions" and started asking me questions about my parenting and lifestyle, like if we smoke in the house (I don't smoke). She completely disregarded the reasons why we brought him in. All she did was order a nebulizer with steroids for him. The next day, I asked the nurse if he would be getting an MRI or ECG. She said the pediatrician never ordered those tests. I showed her his face and asked her what it looked like, and she said it looks like Bell's palsy and it usually goes away.

After two days in the hospital, the pediatrician prescribed him an aero chamber and inhaler to go home with. I figured if they weren't concerned, it must not be a big deal. A year later and my son's face only improved a little bit. He talks very slow out the side of his mouth and slurs his words. His immune system never went back to being what it was prior to vaccines. He is always the first to get sick, the last to get better, and he always gets the worst of it.

After all the damages I saw vaccines inflicted on my children, I vowed to never vaccinate my children again. I began educating myself on my legal rights as a parent over the health and safety of my children. My last two children are completely unvaccinated. They are now seven and nine, and they have never needed antibiotics for anything. They have never had a single developmental delay. They are the perfect picture of health.

I was angry when I found out that there were thousands of parents with the exact same experiences as myself. I was infuriated that the doctors disregarded their children's injuries and justified it as being sacrifices for the "greater good." I knew I had to start speaking out and warning parents of the dangers, and so I did.

My husband's family lives several hours away, so they weren't around to see our daughter vaccine injured. Because of this, when I started speaking out about vaccines, some of them attacked me and tried turning other people in the family against me. I lost several friends I had known almost my whole life over sharing my daughters story.

I knew I needed to find a way to reach more people, so I created a Facebook group I called Informed Decision Canada. I started gathering up like-minded people with similar stories, and we began organizing so we could do what doctors and the health care system were failing to do. I was going to make sure people were receiving proper informed consent, and they were made aware of the risk *before* they enter into any decision regarding vaccines.

Soon after, I organized my first protest/demonstration in Toronto, at Younge and Dundas Square. About 150 people showed up, and we gained many followers that day. After seeing how many people didn't know that there were risks with vaccinating, I knew we had to step up our game to reach more people. I started organizing a rally in Toronto, at Queens Park, on the day of their open house. I contacted like-minded doctors and other influential people in our movement to speak at our rally. We ended up getting some amazing American speakers such as Brandy Vaughan (founder of LearnTheRisk.org), and Wayne Rhode (author of *The Vaccine Court: The Dark Truth of America's Vaccine Injury Compensation Program*), and we reached a lot of people. Our social media groups started growing by the day.

We were gaining such momentum that the number of people seeking vaccine exemptions for school went way up. So much so, that in the fall of 2019, the Chair of the Board of Health Joe Cressy proposed a bill to the Toronto Board of health, to not only take away philosophical and religious exemptions for school, but to add an increased monetary bonus for doctors having high vaccination rates.

I left my house at three in the morning to drive to Toronto to speak at the BOH meeting and oppose the suggested bill. The entire time we spoke, and shared our painful experiences with the TBOH committee, they blatantly ignored us. They gave no eye contact, offered no questions like they all had with the people who spoke in favor of the proposed bill, and they played with their phones. They compared us vaccine hesitant parents, to flat Earthers.

I knew the people who we needed to take us seriously were not, so when I was offered the opportunity to become a plaintiff in a lawsuit challenging the Government of Ontario for its vaccine mandates, I was full in. We, Vaccine Choice Canada, along with our constitutional lawyer, Rocco Galati, announced our lawsuit at a press release in October of 2019, and it is still ongoing.

After the lawsuit was announced, a friend and fellow freedom fighter, Amanda Forbes, asked me to join forces with her to help run Vaxxed Canada, so we could start videoing people sharing their personal vaccine injury stories and start hosting *Vaxxed II* screenings across Canada. When we were securing venues for the screenings, we were met with a lot of opposition. When we would put down the deposit and make the flyer public, we would soon get a call from the venue stating that they had been threatened, and they had to cancel on us.

Many of our screenings had to be kept private, the location revealed only after the person bought a ticket in order to protect our venues so they wouldn't have to cancel on us. One of the venues had said they were threatened by Public Health, which Public Health denied doing.

With the amount of opposition we received, we knew we were making a big impact, so we, Vaxxed Canada/Canadians for Vaccine Choice, started arranging what was going to the biggest freedom fighting rally Canada has seen. We had secured some of the biggest names in our movement to come and speak at Queens Park in Toronto, which was supposed to happen in May of 2020. Then COVID-19 came.

We were told we would have to wait until the stay at home orders were lifted, before they would give us permission/clearance for a legal demonstration to be held on the grounds. We all thought that COVID-19 would be quickly done and over, like with SARS, but it escalated to telling family members they can't see each other, closing down small businesses, and making masks mandatory. I knew immediately they would be coming out with a new vaccine for Covid, and they would socially penalize people who refused to get it.

Courage through the Darkness

I looked into the numbers the media was giving, and then I was hearing from frontline health care workers that the PCR tests were giving false positives. Other deaths that were caused by cancer, heart attack, flu, etc. were being listed as Covid. All the flu deaths that were recorded in the years prior had now coincidentally disappeared, and those same usual numbers were now replaced with COVID-19. I knew something wasn't right, and I wasn't buying their narrative. When Justin Trudeau made the announcement that the Canada Day celebration in Ottawa was cancelled, I was asked to join the many newly formed groups organizing to fight the lockdown and other draconian measures they were forcing on us. We were going to put on our own celebration in civil disobedience.

The night before I was to leave for the demonstration in Ottawa, my husband and I were told the tragic news that my father-in-law was diagnosed with pancreatic cancer. I had several people depending on me to carpool with, and I had agreed to do live videos of the demonstration for Vaxxed Canada. My husband suggested I continue with my plans anyway, as it wasn't going to change anything. Or so we thought.

The following morning, all hell broke loose. My husband started receiving angry phone calls from his family, telling him that because I went to Ottawa, he was not allowed to see his father until he quarantined for two weeks. Because of how they were shutting everything down for Covid, my father-in-law was too late to receive the test for his early diagnoses, so he started declining fast and was beyond treatment. This only made my husband's family angrier with me. I was publically bullied by them on social media and was accused of doing it on purpose. Because my husband's family were buying into the fear based ideologies surrounding Covid, they were furious that I was defying the rules by not socially distancing myself from people and refusing to wear a mask. I was brutally attacked and slandered by them on social media for speaking out, not complying with social distancing, and for refusing to believe what the media was telling me. I loved my father-in-law very much, and he was very special to me, so being castigated from the family was very hard on me. However, just like I did with vaccines, I knew I had to stand for what I believe in and know is right, regardless of the consequences.

If I have any advice to give, it would be for people to understand, now more than ever, it is imperative to see that this plandemic will not go away until they stop being afraid to think for themselves and stand apart from the majority, even if that means standing alone. Be strong and be brave.

Here are two of my favorite quotes that I feel are so relevant to this time we are in:

"Stand up to hypocrisy. If you don't, the hypocrites will teach. Stand up to ignorance, because if you don't, the ignorant will run free to spread ignorance like a disease. Stand up for truth. If you don't, then there is no truth to your existence. If you don't stand up for all that is right, then understand that you are part of the reason why there is so much wrong in the world." - Suzy Kassem

"Once you reject fear, you will become the perfect candidate to receive and reflect Truth."
— Suzy Kassem

About Amanda Moses:

Amanda Moses is a stay-at-home mom who lives in northern Ontario, Canada, with her husband, five children, and a German Shepherd named Max. She enjoys the country life on her hobby farm where they keep chickens and grow gardens. She homeschools her five children and is a certified makeup artist. She loves cooking and baking for her family and taking long country walks. After experiencing vaccine injuries on her children, it led her to starting vaccine risk awareness groups on social media to make people aware of their rights to informed consent and vaccine exemptions. She has organized several protests and rallies in Toronto to promote vaccine risk awareness, and in October of 2019, through Vaccine Choice Canada, along with four other mothers, she filed a lawsuit against the Government of Ontario challenging the vaccine mandates for school through constitutional lawyer Rocco Galati. She has attended several protests against the COVID-19 lockdown measures.

Chapter Eighteen

Action 4 Canada

By Tanya Gaw

I must admit I was surprised when I was asked to share my story. An ordinary Canadian, mother of two, goes activist! What an honour and a privilege to be given the opportunity to tell my story and how Action4Canada began.

I was brought up in a Christian home and went to church. I had a good childhood. I have a sister, Mariah, and a twin brother, Rob, and we were blessed to have our mom home raising us and a dad who worked hard to provide. Both my parents immigrated to Canada and were so grateful to live here. Within a month of arriving in Canada, my mom and her family signed up for English lessons, which they paid for themselves. My parents never received a dime from the government, but that did not stop them from flourishing. In fact, it made them stronger. Their contribution to society, the community, and Canada as a whole was richer for it. They instilled in their children a strong work ethic and a love for this country.

But it is the gift of faith in God that was transformational in my own life and created the warrior within me today. Through some really tough trials and years of hardship, my faith and tenacity grew. Apart from God I was a shell of a person, but with Him I believed I could move mountains. Matthew 17:20: Jesus told them, "I tell you the truth, if you had faith even as small as a mustard seed, you could say to this mountain, "Move from here to there and it would move. Nothing would be impossible."

I began to pray to have faith the size of that mustard seed because I knew this was the only way to overcome the darkness that was entering our land. Prior to the COVID-19 narrative being unleashed upon Canadians, we were already under great threat of losing our sovereignty. In fact, my own journey of activism began when I started to wake up in 2015 leading up to Justin Trudeau being elected Prime Minister of Canada. I could see the writing on the wall, so to speak, and knew instinctively and without a doubt, that our nation would be experiencing the greatest threat in the history of this country. I also became aware at this time that Canada had already been under attack for many years, decades even, and the target was our most valuable asset, our Judeo-Christian roots.

You see, what Canadians had lost sight of was their history, as they were being conditioned over the years into believing that Canada was no longer a Judeo-Christian nation but a secular one. Secularism, however, is one small step away from tyranny. This was proven shortly after Justin Trudeau was in office when he proclaimed that Canada was the "first post-national state with no core identity." But you can be guaranteed that a country cannot exist without an identity, and Justin Trudeau made it clear he would finish what his father began and fill that void by turning Canada into a communist state. Justin Trudeau's admiration for the Chinese dictatorship is no secret, but Canadians were too apathetic and busy with their own lives to care.

It wasn't until the extreme and unprecedented emergency measures in response to so-called COVID-19 struck that people finally began to wake up and take note.

Many people would say that COVID-19 was the worse thing to ever happen to Canadians, but I would tend to disagree. It was actually a gift and God being merciful in turning humanity back to Him. Canadians had taken their freedoms for granted and had no idea anymore from whence they came.

With the incursion of multi-culturalism in the early 1980's, Pierre Elliot Trudeau knew exactly what this meant for the future of Canada, as it was a strategic part of his plan to divide this nation and destroy the foundation our forefathers had fought and died for. For this reason, multi-culturalism has become known worldwide as a failure if the host countries' values are not being embraced. Canada is at a critical turning point in getting back to our roots. What is our foundation?

Canada is founded on Judeo-Christian biblical principles, inherited through our British Commonwealth and embedded in our Magna Carta. It forms our laws and our values and is a system of governance that sets us apart from totalitarian, extremist, and communist regimes. It gives individuals the right to believe, or not to believe, without fear of persecution, oppression, or even death.

It is critical that Canadians defend their heritage because any other nation governed by different religious or political values is living under oppression. This is why, throughout the so-called pandemic, the global cabal focused their targeted attack on persecuting the church and turning citizens against them. Christianity is the basis for democracy and freedom and is the only thing standing in the way of the free world and complete tyranny.

If you are shocked by this statement, then I would challenge you to further consider whether or not you would give up Canada to live in one of the 57 Muslim majority countries, North Korea, China, Pakistan, or India. The majority of people living in other nations, ruled by any other system of governance or belief, are living under oppression and tyranny.

I would say this is a compelling argument for rising up in defense of this nation's heritage. Whether you believe and have faith as a Christian, or you are a non-believer, you are blessed by living here. Can I get a Patriotic "Hoorah" and "Amen" in agreement?

Coming to the realization of all of this is where a bigger part of my journey began. In 2016, God called me to proclaim Canada as a Christian nation. I always think back and have a chuckle because I had about a dozen people on my email list and no platform whatsoever. But, in a step of faith (mustard seed size), I responded with what would become two of the most important words I would ever come to use on a consistent basis – "Yes, Lord." From then on, doors began to open. Through a leap of faith and a step of obedience, I accepted one opportunity after another to write and speak and use my voice to expose the lies and profess the truth.

This is how Action4Canada began. It started with letters and petitions in response to the many concerning policies the liberals were pushing through the House of Commons as a majority government. Motions and bills such as Bill C-16 (allowing biological men into women's private spaces, as well as compete in women's sports), Motion M-103 (prohibiting criticism of Islam), Bill C-45 (legalization of marijuana making it more accessible to youth), and Bill C-75 (an amendment to the criminal code to soften the laws on crime), etc.

The letter writing campaign started with a small email list of my friends and family and grew into a list of tens of thousands. The campaign consisted of educating others and then equipping them with a letter they could sign and send to the government, local MP's, mayors, and city councilors, as well as the media.

As the "call to action" campaigns expanded, I began to reach out to other groups to seek their expertise on different issues. When Motion M-103 was tabled in the House in 2017, I reached out to Valerie Price, the National Director for ACT! for Canada, who was working tirelessly to warn of the extreme threat political Islam posed on Western Nations. Since meeting in 2017, Valerie and I began to work more closely together. As time passed, the multiple issues of concern began to reveal a common thread: the UN and a globalist cabal. In 2018, I met Mac Rogerson and through shared goals and common interests to protect Canadians' charter rights and freedoms, we also began to work together. In March of 2019, I decided to expand the call to action campaigns and founded Action4Canada, along with the help of Mac and Valerie. The organization was registered in August of 2019 and officially launched in February of 2020.

Action4Canada was created as a grassroots movement reaching out to millions of Canadians and uniting our voices in opposition to the destructive policies tearing at the fabric of this nation. Through the call to action campaigns, we educate, encourage, and equip citizens with the tools they need to take action. We are committed to protecting faith, family, and freedom.

The writing campaigns and petitions A4C launched were in direct response to government legislation undermining our Constitution, Charter Rights, and values founded on Judeo-Christian biblical principles.

The Global Compact on Migration and Sustainable Development Goals (destroying our resources, borders, economy, etc. and handing control to the global bankers and globalist oligarch elites) laid the groundwork for the government to use COVID-19 to drive Canada into a communist-socialist state by destroying our economy and making citizens completely financially reliant on the government. Law enforcement was used to subdue Canadians and unwittingly assist the government's diabolical plan.

In response to all of this, Action4Canada felt we needed to have an even greater impact in defending the rights of Canadians, so we decided to take the organization a step further by engaging in a constitutional legal action against the BC and federal government. This was in response to their extreme abuse of power, using the Emergency Measures as a means to do so.

At a rally on September 13th, 2020, I made the announcement that A4C had agreed to retain the services of Rocco Galati, a top constitutional lawyer, who was willing to take on the defense of our Charter of Rights and Freedoms in response to the extreme and destructive emergency measures of BC Bill 19. Bill 19 was described by other constitutional lawyers as the most draconian legislation they had ever seen, and it needed to be opposed.

After this announcement, Action4Canada began to grow exponentially as fellow Canadians began to step forward and volunteer their time to assist. We quickly grew from a team of three to six, and by the spring of 2021, we had over thirty-five volunteers on the core team.

We launched and stabilized many tactical campaigns and webinars for small businesses, the churches, parents/children, frontline workers/law enforcement, etc. These actions proved to be successful and had a significant and measured impact.

In closing, as one last point of interest, I was very aware from the beginning of this so-called pandemic that it was part of a staged event to gain control of the masses in order to expedite the Global Agenda. I was in the midst of writing a detailed report, *"Government Corruption and Colluding with a Foreign Syndicate,"* when I decided to visit three local hospitals and record the empty tents outside and the "empty" emergency rooms. The previous evening, the MSM was reporting line-ups outside and hospitals were full. I added the evidence to my report, then launched a call to action letter writing campaign requesting everyone write to every single premier and demand they lift the lockdowns, get Canadians back to work, read the report, and commence an investigation against the federal government. Over two hundred emails were sent and not one single premier stepped up to defend the citizens of their province.

This information is evidence that every one of these leaders, along with their health officers, are complicit to treason and should stand trial for crimes against humanity along with every MLA and MP who remained silent. It is critical Canadians become actively involved and support candidates who share our values. They need your time, money, and encouragement.

This book is an historical account of courageous souls who rose up in opposition to one of the greatest crimes against humanity, on a global scale, that the world has ever witnessed. But every single Canadian who volunteered their time to organize or attend rallies, wrote letters, signed petitions, and blasted out the truth via social media, deserve equal credit.

I dedicate this chapter to my amazing mom, Alida Gaw, who at eighty years old would clean my house, pick up groceries, and make me meals so I could put the kind of time in that was necessary to build this organization. I want to thank my sister and my adult children, Matt and Amy, for their support. Valerie and Mac for your never-ending encouragement and support in helping to build Action4Canada. My friend JoeMar for keeping my computers running and secure, and the many volunteers who put in long hours and gave so freely of their time for the cause. I also want to give my Uncle Ed a big shout out because from a young age he repeatedly said to me, "the squeaky wheel gets the attention." These words inspired me to keep writing, calling, rallying, and shouting from the mountaintops. Canada is a Judeo-Christian nation, and this means everything.

So get out there my friends and be squeaky. My sincere hope is that you, too, will be inspired to do great things. It starts with two simple words – "Yes, Lord."

Thank you. God bless you, and God bless Canada.

Tanya Gaw

"Courage is contagious, knowledge is power. You have it, so share it."

About Tanya Gaw:

Tanya Gaw is a committed Christian and defender of faith, family, and freedom. She was born and raised in Canada. Tanya's parents were immigrants from England and the Netherlands. They were very grateful to live in Canada, and they instilled in her a deep love for their nation. She has two adult children, a son and a daughter.

Tanya is the founder of Action4Canada, a grassroots, not-for-profit organization committed to upholding the Canadian Constitution and the Charter of Rights and Freedoms.

Her greatest mission is to declare that Canada is founded on Judeo Christian principles, which were inherited through our British Commonwealth and embedded in our Magna Carta, forming our laws and values. It is a system of governance that sets us apart from totalitarian, extremist, and communist regimes. Because of it, we have the freedom to believe, or not to believe, without fear of persecution and even death.

The "foundation" of democratic governments is under attack because tyrannical forces cannot reign where the rule of law and democracy exist.

Action4Canada.com

Chapter Nineteen

Freedom Thinkers and Common Law Warrior

By Elena Mensch Butler

GROWING UP

I was born and raised in beautiful North Vancouver, British Columbia, with my parents and younger brother. My father was born and raised In Ecuador. During my entire childhood, he worked at Hotel Vancouver as bell captain and guest services manager. My mother was born and raised in Washington State and moved to West Vancouver when she was twelve years old. While she raised us, she was a stay-at-home mom and operated a daycare in our home and hosted exchange students. It was a fun upbringing. I had wonderful friends on my block whom I spent most of my time with. I started off in French emersion, then switched to an English school halfway through primary school. For grade eight and nine, I attended a boarding school in St. Louis, Missouri, before returning home to complete high school. Unfortunately, I had to return home in order to pursue legal action against my maternal grandfather for sexually abusing me during the first four years of my life. My maternal grandmother was also charged for aiding and abetting the abuse. I started to suffer from suppressed memories during the last semester of grade nine. It was then that I experienced the unjust court system as a rape victim, when my millionaire Masonic grandfather allegedly paid off the

The Brave: Courage During COVID in Canada

West Vancouver Crown prosecutor to drop the criminal case. He also paid specialists to lie against me in a ten-year civil case that ended up going nowhere due to his financial power and unexpected death due to health difficulties. My mother and one of her brothers were disinherited for standing up to them. It was this experience that made me the strong woman I am today.

I attended Capilano University for a Bachelor of Tourism Management with a minor in Outdoor Recreation Management and Business. I enjoyed playing sports starting at a young age including softball, skiing, track and field, volleyball, and soccer. By the time I was fourteen I began competing in snowboarding, followed by training with the Canadian National Team, trying out for the 1998 Olympics, instructing and coaching for twenty-six years, and designing kids snowboarding schools for multiple resorts locally and abroad. My travels began at age seventeen, with my first overseas trip without my family on an exchange program to the Philippines. The six-week exchange abroad and yearlong project was sponsored by the YMCA and the Canadian International Development Association. I had attended the Vancouver YMCA Leadership program and conferences all through high school. At the end of the exchange program, I co-authored a book with the other participants. My writing career continued by working for a variety of newspapers throughout my life. I travelled and worked overseas for many years instructing snowboarding and teaching English. I was always interested in business starting around four years old, trying to sell anything I could to the neighbours and family members as a child. In my mid-twenties I opened a tour company that operated until the 2008 recession, and the 2010 Olympics affected it. Throughout my adulthood I spearheaded and attempted multiple different types of businesses while maintaining my snowboarding career. Currently, I own four small businesses with my best friend, my husband of nine years. We live in the countryside of Squamish with our two young boys, who we homeschool.

I do not consider myself religious and I will not label myself, however, I've had my fair share of exploring. I grew up in church and when I was older, I studied a variety of religions and faiths periodically for two decades before taking a lengthy break. Nothing ever sat well for me for a long time, but I always turned to God for my spiritual support. Although I participated in a party lifestyle for an extensive time in my life, suffering from addictions, I believe my love and faith in God always protected me through my travels, dark times, and when I experienced depression due to the sexual abuse and numerous losses due to deaths and a failed business.

SPEAKING OUT

I was always outspoken and strongheaded throughout my life. I had no problem speaking my mind and against anything unfair. I believe it was because of the unjust experiences my family endured in the past. When I was a teenager, a member of my family was severely injured by the tetanus vaccine with side effects of seizures. My mother has been awake to the corruption of vaccines and the deep state since I was a child. After my family member was injured and my godson was killed by a vaccination in the Philippines, I started to become conscious to the pharmaceutical industry venality. When I was in university, the tragedy of 9/11 occurred. I subsequently witnessed Coca-Cola unexpectedly take over funding of my university and dictate the curriculum. As time rolled on, the global and corporate corruption caught my attention. I had already witnessed the suspicious dishonesty in other nations during my travels. In my twenties I started to speak out against vaccinations, but of course I received a lot of resistance from society in response. However, I still pursued warning others about the dangers of the side effects and deaths, which were rarely reported and was suppressed by the global media. During the majority of my outspoken years, I was only supported by my parents. In my thirties I began to meet like-minded friends who shared the same information and beliefs. My community then began to grow. When my husband and I met, he knew about the deep state but did not realize the extent of how evil it was. I was extremely fortunate that he was open-minded because his family was pro-vaccine and only believed information relayed by the media. Over the ten years of our relationship, my spouse grew and became quite educated despite being ridiculed by his family, especially over our decision to not vaccinate our children and to homeschool. Before having children, we were already aware of the indoctrination of the public school system. Our children attended Waldorf for their pre-school years before we decided to homeschool with a distance learning private school in January 2020.

MY PANDEMIC AWARENESS

When the COVID-19 pandemic signs began in November of 2019, I was suspicious it was fake. As I mentioned previously, I was educated and aware of the deep state strategies, adrenochrome, the pharmaceutical corruption, Bill Gates COVID-19 patents and his plans to depopulate Earth, the Georgia Guidestones, human trafficking, child sex slavery, the former planned shootings, the false media brainwashing the masses, the previous phoney viruses and pandemics, the indoctrination of our schools, the illegal banking system created by the Rothchild's, and the families that not only controlled our planet, but also funded our wars on both sides for hundreds of years. I was fortunate that my mother was awake for majority of her life, and she planted seeds of education in my mind and taught me how to critically think. As a teenager, I loved studying entrepreneurship. I became interested in following Donald Trump and read all his books. Then I listened to them when they became available on CD. One of my favorites was *The Art of the Deal*, which taught me negotiation skills, leadership, and management. I later discovered the book was inspired by *The Art of War* by Sun Tzu, which Trump has used as a guide during his war against the Deep State (cabal). Little did I know that twenty years later, my knowledge of Trump and experience meeting him at a business course in Los Angeles would be a huge support for my faith and trust in Trump throughout the pandemic. I supported him in the 2016 election because I knew if Hilary had won, we would have been rounded up into FEMA camps and she would start a war with Russia. I was fully aware of her agenda. It was lonely supporting Trump back then. People had no clue how much danger we were in. I was thrilled to hear that ending human trafficking was in Trump's campaign plans. It was at the beginning of the pandemic that I learned Trump was a key leader in a massive global military operation, referred to as the White Hats, which is eliminating the cabal, human trafficking, and rescuing children and honey pot women from sex slavery. I learned we were experiencing a spiritual war between Satan and God that has been occurring for thousands of years. I also learned that the masks were a symbol of compliance to the cabal and to silence mankind. In addition, my suspicion of the COVID-19 shot as a component of the Agenda 21 plan to depopulate the world, as written on the Georgia Guidestones, was confirmed this year. This was information my mother and I retained over the years from our research and began to make complete sense to both of us.

MY PANDEMIC EXPERIENCE

As the planet proceeded into lockdowns, riots to defund the police force, and experienced unjust political decisions, I was fortunate to reside in a small town that was scarcely affected by the pandemic compared to larger cities and other nations. In March 2020, we progressed into a low-key lockdown for two months with businesses, restaurants, schools, bars, playgrounds, and churches closed. Big box stores remained open, of course, however we were still permitted to play outside freely. Our family businesses immediately started to feel the effect of the economic shift, dropping our revenue by 70%. We fell into deeper debt, and we began to feel a lot of stress. We were worried about losing our home, property, and our businesses which operated from our land. Our mortgage renewal was expiring, and we were being advised to sell. We decided not to, even though we knew if the real estate market dipped the next year, we could lose everything. The mask mandates did not get stricter in our town until fall of 2020. Until this day, I have never worn a mask and never will. As Bonnie Henry, Provincial Health Officer for British Columbia, turned up the heat, the local businesses denied mask exemptions completely. I was bullied in stores by both employees and customers. One time, in a large local grocery store, I was harassed by four employees, resulting in me walking away from a cart load of products. I have never returned. I shifted to online grocery shopping at another grocery store, which I enjoy now. I continued to find retailers for my other family needs that supported my right to not wear a mask. I also walked into big box stores and stood up for my human rights multiple times, and they all allowed me to continue to shop. I never backed down. My husband was the same way with the stores. We both realized it was important for our children's future and our freedom by defying the illegal restrictions and mandates with civilized disobedience. We were well-informed the restraints were against the Canadian Human Rights Act, the Canadian Charter of Rights and Freedoms, and the Nuremberg Code.

FREEDOM THINKERS

In March of 2020, a few local moms and I started a club of families in our town called The Freedom Thinkers, in which I took on the main leadership role of organizing our gatherings and social media connections. I created a Facebook thread and page where we chat about the current global situation and mandates. We share information daily and have become an amazing emotional support for each other. Immediately, during our two month lockdown, we met an average of two to three days a week in person, with our children, for potlucks and socialization. Some days we were together for eight hours. Everyone was off work. We gathered at my home or at another member's property, as we both did not have neighbours close by to report us. We were not intended to host friends or family at our residences, as per Bonnie Henry. Our group grew with locals throughout the Sea the Sky corridor, and families joined us from the city. We attended freedom rallies and marches together in Vancouver City throughout the year. A thread was created on Facebook and later Telegram for international members and Canadians outside of our area. Another Freedom Thinker group branched off and was created in Vancouver City. Later, a chapter started up in Alberta. Between all the groups we now have a membership base of 500 families. After the summer, we continued to meet at my property on weekends, including hosting a Christmas party with over sixty adults and children. That evening at 6:30 pm, during dinner, the police came to our door and handed us a $2300 fine for disobeying the no guest restrictions. The officers informed me we had to either send our visitors home immediately or receive a fine. When I inquired if they intended on returning that evening if I accepted the fine, they replied they would not. That immediately indicated to me the fine was not about health but rather just a government money grab.

COMMON LAW
Shortly after receiving the illegal fine, I was introduced to an amazing team in Vernon, British Columbia (BC), who were assisting Canadians dispute their fines and won. The leaders taught me to write "refuse for cause, no contract" across the front of the ticket, take a picture of it, and return it to the dispute address on the back. The ticket never returned to me. I had won. I was inspired. I began attending their weekly zoom meetings to learn more about common law. I posted about my win on Facebook publicly, and in response I ended up helping Canadians across the nation dispute and win their fines. Canada has always been operating under common law. Our courts are illegally operating under maritime law. I soon joined the Common Law Grand Jury. The team has sent out three warnings to end restrictions, followed by subpoenas, to 166 government officials including: all BC mayors, Bonnie Henry, Adrian Dix, and the attorney general of Canada and BC. I began assisting with our campaigning to the public for the education zoom calls and expanding the grand jury, through social media and by recently speaking at the Vancouver World Freedom Rally in March 2021. Once we complete the prosecutions in BC, we will be conducting

the same process for every Canadian province. We hope to inspire other countries to do the same. We have already begun to team up with a common law group in Australia and reaching out to other Commonwealth nations in order to encourage them to follow our steps.

EDUCATION WARRIOR – HOW I WAS AFFECTED

Recently, I trained Freedom Thinker members to educate our local businesses about the mask exemptions blue sheet information written by the BC human rights commissioner. I had received the guidance from the Hugs Over Masks leadership team. For the past few weeks, I have been emailing the information to managers of stores I know, who have been grateful and responded well. I have also joined the BC team for the Canadian Chapter of the Children's Health Defence, spearheaded by Robert F. Kennedy, to combat against mandatory vaccinations in Canada.

My journey this year has included countless hours of my husband and I educating ourselves regarding this spiritual war we are currently enduring, as there are so many components attached to it. We became digital warriors. Every night we researched and listened to documentaries or podcasts by light workers instead of watching television. In return, I spent endless hours, days, and months educating others who have approached me for information and comfort for their pain as they woke up to the truth. Our favorite documentaries to share with new learners were *Out of the Shadows* and *Fall of the Cabal*. I have been told by others on an ongoing basis this year that I have been a rock and an amazing source of knowledge combined with strong faith. I have tried to inform friends and acquaintances all year, planting seeds along the way. Some have listened. Some have ignored me and dumped me. I have been ostracised and publicly shamed on community Facebook groups. I was booted off our local moms Facebook group for posting about the human trafficking industry before being bullied by an administrator and told I needed mental health assistance on a thread with over 3000 members to read. I was banned on Facebook multiple times. I lost friendships I had since my childhood and high school years. We have experienced loss of business opportunities for standing up and for putting more time into combating and educating this past year. We risked our home and property, in which our businesses also operate from. We incurred more debt. We have sacrificed time away from our children. We were constantly cleaning up the house before and after gatherings. Plus contributing food to the potlucks. We put off personal and work projects. We exhausted my parents, who graciously assisted with our sons during our hard-working hours. We have not taken a full day off to relax, hit the ski hill, or time for ourselves all year. Not one family vacation together. Even when we went camping in the summer once, we were working or educating. We sacrificed and put a lot on the line in defiance of the COVID-19 illegal restrictions, mandates, and regulations. Our belief was that truth seekers and educators do not ask for funds; therefore, our volunteer work was for free out of the goodness of our hearts and to fight for freedom. God always provided because we are on his side.

COURAGE

It took a lot of strength and courage for my husband and me to stand up for what was right this past year, even though numerous powers were working against us. Our marriage was tested, only to become stronger. Meanwhile, we witnessed relationships and marriages fall apart around us. Yes, we are exhausted, but we know we have fought for the future of all children as much as we could this past year. We have helped so many families connect during a time when we were supposed to be separated. We created a safe environment to socialize, preventing adults and children from experiencing loneliness and possible mental health issues. We gained and created friendships with real, amazing, like-minded people among our community. Friends we would have never met before this pandemic. We are incredibly grateful for that. My husband and I grew so much over the past year together. Our minds and values shifted. We grew spiritually. My faith in God has never been stronger. I gained peace in my heart that I have never felt before. I quit bad habits that ruled over me for majority of my life. I gained self-love and self-respect. I learned new boundaries. I let go of unhealthy friendships. My children and I began to attend Sunday school so they could learn more about God and his love for us. My children learned a lot about the world and are aware of the current global situation and the deep state. They learned to become critical thinkers at an incredibly young age. I believe I was conditioned for this time because of experiencing the sexual abuse and unjust court system, waking up to the corruption at an early age, battling and overcoming addictions, gaining leadership and public speaking abilities, and developing a relationship with God. It is these aptitudes and experiences that brought me to the mindset and put the fire in my belly that I needed to take the leadership action to stand up for the rights and freedoms of humanity.

I have always believed that the current global situation is an ancient spiritual war between God and Satan, dating back thousands of years. What we are experiencing is biblical, and so much more information that has been hidden to us is about to be released to the world.

The Brave: Courage During COVID in Canada

Unfortunately, many who have chosen not to pay attention in the past could die. Especially from the vaccine. This is a war. In wars there are always casualties and injuries. I am grateful for my faith in God, in Trump's leadership, and the White Hat Global Military team that is eliminating the cabal and ending human trafficking. I am grateful for my connections, mentors, and for the light workers who have kept me informed as well as lifted my spirits so I could help others. I am grateful to my parents and my husband for all their support during this journey. I am not a super woman and not perfect. I have had my bad days, too. I could not have achieved my activism this past year without a lot of assistance. Although I believe God and the White Hat's are going to expose the corruption to all humanity soon, there is still a lot of work ahead of us. We will have people struggle with the information that will be revealed. They will need love and support. There will be decades of healing to be completed emotionally and physically. There will be a lot of unlearning to be processed as mankind discovers how we have been indoctrinated, brainwashed, and lied to our entire lives. I encourage everyone to prepare themselves for this upcoming journey. The souls of truth seekers, revealers, and healers chose to be here for this amazing time on Earth. We were placed all around the earth on purpose to help others. Get strong in body, soul, and mind. Educate yourselves so you can be there for others, especially for the family and friends who have outcast you like a black sheep. Allow yourself to feel anger and to process it. There will be good days and bad days. That is okay. Attend the rallies and marches to help wake up the masses. Do not be afraid to speak up. Join a team that is making a difference in this world. My choice was to join the Common Law Grand Jury to prosecute and hold those accountable for siding with the wrong side of this war. Educate businesses with the proper signage for mask exemptions. Be alert and be ready for what is coming. We are in the Great Awakening. God has won this war; however, he is waiting for us all to have the courage to unite and stand up for our freedom.

"Have the heart of a lion, the skin of a rhino, and the soul of an angel." -Author Unknown

About Elena Mensch Butler:

Elena Mensch Butler is the founder of The Freedom Thinkers, a Common Law Grand Jury member, a member of the British Columbia Children's Health Defense team and has been an avid educator and digital warrior during the COVID-19 pandemic. Elena grew up in North Vancouver, British Columbia, and now resides with her husband and two young boys in Squamish. She spent most of her life traveling, coaching, and competing in the snowboard industry. When she is not on the mountain, her passion is to write, public speak, collect pets, and play outdoors with her family. She and her spouse now own multiple businesses and a hobby farm, as well as homeschool their sons. Elena attended university for a Bachelor of Tourism Management, Outdoor Recreation Management, and Business. Her current goal in life is to support and encourage humanity as we all wake up to claim our rights and freedoms.

Chapter Twenty

Following the Heart of Lyberty

By Kaja Gjesdal

In 2016 my whole world started to crumble when my partner started to go crazy. Our family's protector was losing his mind and his body, so I had to learn how to connect deeply with the soul. I believed the power of my love could save him. My learning was that we can only save ourselves, and we must heal to also save our children.

My little girl and I arrived back in Vancouver, Canada, from my studies in South America on March 16th, one day before Argentina shut down its borders because of the COVID-19 virus. We had been traveling on my vision quest for a year.

Since early January 2020 we were in Mar Del Plata, Argentina, to help a friend with her healing. I was training in the tantric art of belly dancing and meeting in Peru with a doctor of Shamanism. It felt like the virus started following me at the end of February, when the bus ride after ours in Buenos Aires had an outbreak, and a waterfall hike we missed by a day in the Amazon was connected to another carrier.

The Brave: Courage During COVID in Canada

The plan when we came back had been to stay with my mother until Lyberty finished her grade one school year with other children, and I would start working and get a home in the summer where Lyberty wanted to settle. But schools were closed until September, and she had no kids to play with in the small town we were in. Being raised with a stepfather and mother deeply connected to CBC news, my belief in the "plandemic" caused a huge divide over what the world was experiencing. Lyberty and I were out on our own by June to find our way through the chaos. There was a separation from my family; the universe had other plans for us.

A seer I've been working with for years told me I would soon come upon a time of deep realization of what it means to be a part of what society called "privileged." I didn't know how my future was going to unfold, but my first instinct was to stock up on food. I needed to find some purposeful work, and our sanctuary, as soon as possible.

I didn't know where we belonged after I had to sell our home in Kelowna in 2019. I just knew I had to live with courage and continue to trust that our hearts would lead us. After so much travelling, I had promised Lyberty it was her turn to heal, and to show me where we would make a home. She had developed an addiction to socializing over the screen with friends via video games and online learning months before there were any lockdowns. I needed to find a community and a healthier environment for her development.

One of the rules at the time of the first lockdown was that we could only be around family we lived with, so we tried to root back in Kelowna with her grandparents and cousins on her father's side. There was still a lot of healing in the family after the traumatic loss of Sasha, but I felt I was ready to assist. I had a positive relationship with Lyberty's grandmother and felt that Lyberty would be the bridge to the healing of hearts. For a short time we were happy to be living back in Kelowna starting over, but this too was not where we were meant to be … yet.

There was what I now call "trauma drama," the triggering within someone's nervous system of past unhealed wounds. After some confusion around bullying language of with our children, her cousins were taken away because of this wound activation from the other mother.

For three days Lyberty expressed her agony in painful cries. "I want to die; I don't want to suffer anymore. I want to be with daddy." Her heart was broken again. I had shared with her a teaching about the death of her father, that his body had to leave us because it was suffering too much. This is how she connected to her finding a way out of her own, for the body to die.

As her mother, this rocked me to my core. She started having dreams again of being taken by men in uniform coming from the walls. She didn't feel safe back in this world. With her father not here to protect us with his physical presence, I was going to have to become the warrior I knew I had been training to become. My Vision Quest had led us back to where it had started, and now we were homeless during a world "pandemic." We left as soon as we could, this time trusting a new friend with a son Lyberty's age who was living on Salt Spring Island.

I could hear her father's spirit say, "Follow Lyberty's heart." I had to put the oxygen mask on my child first. I didn't really know anyone on the island, and I hadn't worked since her dad had gotten sick. My focus had been on my healing and studies for the past four years. I would now have to find work during a lockdown on a small little island. Here I was with all of this wisdom to share in a new community I had never lived in. How was I going to find the work I had been preparing to do, where I barely knew anyone and no community groups or gatherings was allowed? I was a yogi and used my breath work to stay connected to my energy and nervous system. I refused to wear a mask, for I knew it wasn't healthy for those working with PTSD triggers. Where could I work in the public? I had to surrender and to trust.

Salt Spring was magical. There were barely any masks walking around, and no playgrounds with caution tape. A family we grew close to felt a bond with us as soon as Lyberty walked in the door. The mother and I could sense the spiritual connection between my daughter and the daughter they had lost a few months before Lyberty was born. We felt immediate love, acceptance, and joy again. There was a deep soul connection. Lyberty was free to be, and her happiness filled up both of our hearts. We even found space in a small private school in the forest with an outdoor classroom. It was a summer of singing and dancing on the beaches. Her playful spirit started coming back, and she was living out the meaning of the sound of her name ... *freedom*. She was off the screen and playing in nature. Somehow, I had to make this work.

Continuing my studies of Tibetan medicine online, I kept myself open to ways of making a future for us. There was joy in the days of picking olives in the orchards, but nothing for me ended up flowing long enough. I tried building connections online for life coaching but felt a disconnection through a computer. I wanted to hug and hold the people I was helping. Hold circles, not Zoom meetings.

I was running out of my savings quickly; all of my privileges were drying up. My car broke down, I had to stop doing my hair, slow down on my supplement purchases, stop any shopping, and live as cheaply as we could. I had to start making money now. Focus was the name of this game. I knew I had to continue my sacred practices and trust in my co-creation with the universe. Something had to happen to help us out of this confusion. "Please," I prayed. "Please show me how to do this." I asked this of my inner guidance, my angels for assistance. My cannabis and psilocybin use were increasing again. The stress, anxiety, and depression were slowly creeping in. Living on the island was getting to me, but Lyberty was so happy and she felt at home.

In November, a magical new friend offered to pay for me to take part in a tribal grief ritual he felt I was meant to attend. I was curious about this healing method, was missing some community, and couldn't turn down a gift, so I committed to the weekend ceremony. I don't know how to fully explain what happened, but what I ended up connecting to on a very deep level was the energy of "loss of tribe" – the loss of unconditional love and safety in the family unit. I felt it for my own lived experience and for the collective. I was so emotionally, physically, and spiritually depleted from it, that by Monday, I received my bleeding cycle weeks early and started to not feel well for the first time I could remember. The call came mid-week that someone in the group had tested positive for COVID-19. I was told to self-isolate for two weeks and asked if I would get tested. I felt it would be best I stay home for that time to make sure, but I didn't see a need to get tested.

I believe in common sense. If I don't feel well, I am going to slow down and help my body heal so I get better no matter what. This virus had a 98% survival rate. As someone who has been practicing alternative medicine for years and doesn't get sick, I wasn't worried that I would die from how I felt. If all else fails, then I will knock on the doors of western medicine.

Knowing how powerful our mind is over our body, I decided not to alarm the other people I was living with because I know part of manifesting anything is thinking about it. I didn't want to contribute to the psychological abuse of fear energy and would monitor closely my health and those I was living with.

The truth was I couldn't breathe deeply into my lungs. Every morning for the past three years I have had meditation practices with deep breathing. I had definitely caught something and now had a symptom linked to the COIVD-19 virus I could work with. I truly believe everything does happen for a reason, and I was being tested to use the tools I had been studying to finally use on my physical body in disease. I am making no claim that I have any cures, but I did truthfully get better every day and was back to myself completely after the two-week isolation rule.

Here is some of what I did:

~ Use medicinal cannabis in smoke and edible form for anti-inflammatory, bronchial dilation, and relaxing of nervous system.

Following the Heart of Lyberty

~ Immerse the body in a hot bath with water up to the neck to allow heat and steam to loosen lungs.
~ Sing healing mantras that loosen lungs with powerful vibrations and deep breathing.
~ Increase the use of healing herbs and teas for the lungs like Echinacea.
~ A teaspoon of Manuka honey everyday
~ Stay positive in thoughts and outlook.
~ Keep dancing and laughing, stay connected to joyful activities.
~ Sleep well
~ Eat lots of healthy vegetarian based soups and bone broth.

By Christmas time I was completely broke and feeling broken. The PTSD cycle I had just spent three years healing was starting to surface again. I wasn't sleeping well and kept having the feeling that if I stayed, we would die. I could end up on the streets and lose rights to my little girl. If we left Salt Spring, it would break Lyberty's heart. How could I do that to her? My prayers had to get stronger, my meditation deeper.

Just as I was starting to run out of food and had told my mother I may have to go to the food bank, I got a message while looking for work in Vancouver that an adult at Lyberty's school tested positive for COVID-19. The school was shutting down until the new year. It was the sign I was looking for; it was time to pack up and leave the island, maybe for good. Without Lyberty's school, there was nothing holding us to stay.

We left in the middle of the night with whatever my car could fit. I had no idea where we were going to stay, but I knew we had to leave to live. A wise Indigenous elder who had been helping me to understand my spiritual path of transformation was there to help us; an angel had arrived. The first night we slept in a hostel in Squamish; the next night we found an apartment, suite 111; a magical sign. A mutual friend with similar visions of helping others heal with plant medicines had similar work ideas through non-profits. Prayers answered again, we weren't going to be on the streets. We had a place to live and people to work with. I really wanted to be able to assist people with what they needed to get through this transitional time.

That Christmas was the first time I had ever spent the holiday without family and one of my daughters. My eldest was with her boyfriend and his family. I had no money to spend on gifts or to see my family. My focus needed to be on work now that I was living back in Vancouver.

I had to make the hard choice of sending Lyberty to stay with her dad's family, who had taken me to court after he died but had the money and stability to give her the kind of holidays she deserved. The mother who had broken her heart before offered to be with her, to transform the pain they were still carrying in their hearts. It was the only gift I needed. My sacrifice was worth her happiness.

Soon into the new year of 2021, things started to shift more into an abundant flow. The non-profit I was aligning with was presented with a food donation program. I didn't have to worry about being able to buy food anymore and had a service we could connect and build with others. After a few weeks, and my trying again to homeschool and keep her off screens, Lyberty started having dreams of the island calling her back. When she told me she missed her school and friends more than her daddy, I had to reach out. The mother who had felt a connection to her heart as soon as she met her offered to look after her during school days until the year was finished. We found our tribe, our family. What blessings; I could work in Vancouver and be with Lyberty on weekends. I miss her all the time, and we talk almost every day. It's been really hard on us both, but I know we are meant to be where we are right now for our future. I remind Lyberty how strong she is, about being brave, and tell her we are warriors. We have the power of love on our side. It's all around us and never dies.

As I am writing this, I received a message from another new friend in alignment with a non-profit: "I prayed for the right people to help achieve something special." Me too, my new friend. Me too. The work I am now doing in the downtown eastside of Vancouver is connected to a vision I had years ago when I started my healing path with teacher plants. Helping those who are suffering most in their addictions from trauma, especially our First Nations where I live. With mental health issues on the rise, and our need to connect back with caring for our Mother Earth, this is where I know I am meant to do the work I have been studying for. This is the vision my father told me was important to connect with when I was only a little girl myself – to support the healing and raising up of Indigenous Peoples, so we can all heal from the roots of the pains from colonization. The rewilding of us *all*.

I know soon we will also find our home together, my Lyberty and me. The stars just have to align. Maybe during the summer where we both dance wild and free as happy as can be.

My message is to trust we are being guided by an energy, a vibration that is the most powerful of all ... the consciousness of love. Be brave with your hearts and make love to the world.

"Like a Chinese bamboo tree being planted and watered daily, it may take five years to see its growth from all the work being done beneath the soil, but with patience and faith, that tree with its foundation fully rooted, will be able to bend through storms but will not break."

Love, Kaja

About Kaja Gjesdal:

Kaja Gjesdal is a practitioner of the arts of tantra, the consciousness of love.

After the death of her partner and the father of her two daughters in 2017, the need for her to heal the PTSD she was triggered into led her to deep learning of the wellness of body, mind, and soul.

For the past five years she has been studying the ancient ways of healing through Shamanic, Tibetan, Vedic, and First Nation rituals and plant medicines. A spiritual journey with ayahuasca in 2018 showed her the great suffering of our human history and a rebirth of the blissful state we truly are.

As a mother and a lover, she is dedicated to the healing of hearts, focused at this time on her children's future and the shift of the collective into a new way of living in unity with Mother Earth.

THANK YOU TO THE BRAVE DONORS

So much gratitude for all the donations that were received to help produce and publish this book! Without your support in uncertain times, this book may not have been possible.

If we ever find ourselves in situations where we want to help, we want to do something, but we just don't know how we can make a real impact ... in these times you can never go wrong when you support, encourage, and believe in those who are taking action and making a difference.

When you surround yourself with the warriors of the world, the conversations become very different.

BE BRAVE, DO SOMETHING!

SHERRY ROY	BREANNA WATKINS
KILIE DEWE	JEFF FLOWERDEW
GIANFRANCO BARILLA	PAIGE ANN MCIVOR
CHAR-LEIGH POTVIN	KRISTEN M HOLWELL
BRANDON MURRAY	WELDON FRIESEN
DAMIEN GENDRON	HUNTER COURTE
TANIA KHAZAAL	MELANIE SKRYPNYK
ELENA BUTLER	KIM BERGEN
ALANA PONSONBY	ALICIA JOHNSTON
NICOLE FILER	BRETT TRIMMING
KATHERINE SINHA	SHELBY MACKENZIE
JODI LYNN	JEFFREY ROEHR
	CAITLYN RICHER

About Lionheart Publishing

Lionheart Publishing was conceived by Lani Gelera for the purpose of following her passion and inner guidance with conviction. After walking away from a twenty-year career in TV/film, Lani is dedicated to sharing stories and experiences with others to help them navigate these interesting times with a brave and abundant mindset.

Whenever we speak from the heart and share stories that will inspire and empower others, we are taking courageous action in alignment with our individual path, purpose and guidance.

This book *The Brave: Courage during COVID* is the first volume in a seven-part series meant to connect and empower each of our seven chakras. Volume One is green to attune with the Heart Chakra, since being courageous is an act of love.

More Books By Lionheart Publishing:

The Brave 2: Speaking Truth to Power will be blue to attune with the Throat Chakra with full expression in using our voice to share conscious truth information. This book is under production at the time of this print and projected to be available by July 2021.

The Brave 3: Elevating Human Consciousness will be indigo to attune with the Third Eye Chakra. Projected to come out in September 2021.

Lionheart Activation Journal – 30 Day Journaling Challenge to Build a Brave and Abundant Mindset. For those interested in doing their own personal growth work and developing their conversation with divine intelligence and self. Published and available.

All of these books will be available through Amazon.com and on the Fenix Fallgirl Website at www.fenixfallgirl.com under Lionheart Publishing.